Life of a Salesperson.
Salesperson.
The beginning.

Acknowledgements

The journey, this story tells about, has been excellent, and we say "Thank you" to everyone who has contributed and helped us to take this book from being an idea to becoming a reality. From advices on style to the word images, to recommendations on how to best reflect the stories of real-world sales situations, the assistance given to us has been unique.

Thanks to the salespeople who have shared their stories of success and failure with us. Special thanks to Budimir Kļuvaks, Olga Lesņikoviča-Riņķe, and Pavel Zagrebina, the salespeople of the "Scoro Latvia" team, as well as Inese Kungurova and Rūta Fridrihsone for their relentless optimism and sometimes strange questions about the life and thoughts of salespeople.

Thanks to the first readers, or "beta readers", who gave us their comments on the initial story lines and indicated the good and not so good points. Thank you for your comments, Anna Pavlova, Arnis Strods, Ieva Mūrniece, Līva Veļķere, Māris Veismanis and Ints Valcis.

Kārlis Ozols kindly gave us some book publishing tips, and we say "Thank you" for that.

Thanks to the lovely editor, Zane Ūsele, whose relentless effort has improved the story. Your knowledge and enthusiasm have helped to create a work we can be proud of.

Finally, we say "Thank you" to our loved ones. You have been beside us, watched us as we worked, and supported us when we felt discouraged. You know who you are. Thank you for being with us!

Preface

I love sales! I have worked in sales for 16 years and enjoyed every meeting, every difficult customer, and every product presentation. I have experienced so many sales situations that I could talk about them for days.

A little more than two years ago I had an idea to write a book about sales. It seems everyone, in their own specialist area, thinks about writing a book. So, I ignored this thought for quite a long time, until one day I decided to write. In the beginning it was interesting—for about five pages. Then I realized that there is so much to say, but the book needed structure. I wanted the story to be true, to be real. I did not want my book to be regular textbook about sales, another one of the thousands already existing in the world.

After some time, I was lucky enough to become a part-time sales trainer. I still enjoy training very much, and it has helped me to write this book. A professional sales trainer teaches structure and speaks tirelessly about actual sales issues. Finally, I integrated my knowledge and experience, and realized that I cannot waste them. But how could I share them, so they would reach the readers of my book?

* * * * *

Our company is continually growing, and while conducting a job interview, I found myself sitting opposite of a young woman who was eager to work in the customer assistance department of our company. I had the feeling that she was not the right choice for that particular job, so I asked what she would really like to do. It turned out that she wanted to write. Unfortunately, writing is not a well-paying job in Latvia.

After the interesting interview we shook hands, and Inese had the opportunity to begin her dream job. I, on the other hand, had found the missing magic for my book— a girl who knew nothing about sales and was brave to undertake this experience and share her feelings.

Probation Period: Salespeople Also Cry was written as quickly and easily as giddy cocktail, and share real selling experiences, experiments, emotional experiences, stories, people, places, situations and other sales components imbued with a "magical creative sauce" in the single story that runs through the pages of this book.

As a salesperson, or as a sales trainer, you have an exciting job that will not only delight your imagination, but also involves a lot of hidden, excellent knowledge of the art of sales. Take your time, and I hope that you enjoy this book!

Vigants Lesausks

Author
Sales Trainer, Sales Assistant Team Leader
Winner of Sales Guru, 2007 and Sales Management Guru, 2015

Selling is a story. So, this is the story, about what it means to start something new, and to be afraid of the outcome; and about the assumptions we live with, and how much we could accomplish, if even for a minute, we could forget what "cannot" be done. This is a story about daring to follow the dream. Not only the Maggie's dream, the heroine of this book, but also what is experienced by recording the story from the first word to the last.

I started to write this story in order to find out if I could be a salesperson. In some ways, Maggie's story is a test period for me as well, and for each reader, because at the moment when we make decisions, we have to realize that there are many more challenges than we initially expected. It is clear that this story has allowed me to look at salespeople from a different perspective and allowed me to go into the nuances of sales and exclaim in surprise that we are salespeople in spite of our occupation and our struggles—everyone! And as my singing teacher says, "only the level of our professionalism differs". When we start a new job, begin attending a university, or start new friendships, we sell ourselves. It is our world views and ability to adapt our tool box that will help us to achieve success. The only question is, how skillfully we will do it?

This story is a little bit different, because its author continues learning. It includes cognitions, experience, and moments of insight that flows from Tamm Solutions, and that have been given to me by Vigants Lesausks and his team at Scoro. This story relates the real survival games of salespeople and the huge waves of emotion they experience.

And, I defy you to create your own story, one that reveals your probation period, your art of selling, and shares your experiences. Maggie taught me not to be afraid anymore, and I recommend that to you too!

Inese Mūrniece,
Author

Getting the Job

"I want to sell the world to the world," I say, breathing deeply and tightening my lips in expectation.

Ed Lewis is sitting next to me, serious, with half-closed eyes, as if he is repeating my words in his mind. I pretend not to notice it. I know it is part of the test. "That may sound pompous, but I believe that having ambition allows us to do the work entrusted to us much better!"

"Pompous!" Ed repeats. "And what do you do when your ambitions die down?"

"I work on myself," I tell him, straightening my back. "I'm focused, learn quickly, and I have the ability to adapt to almost any situation. Excitement helps me to overcome any difficulties."

"And then?"

Lewis looks bored, and it upsets me. He sits further back on the bench and focuses on a couple who have decided to eat their breakfast on the park's lawn. It even seems he has forgotten that we are having a job interview, and that it is taking place on this sunlit bench, and not in the office. *Does he really not understand how important this interview is to me?*

"And then?" he repeats, regaining his focus and turning to me.

"I know why I am doing everything. I have dreams, and I'm fighting for them! I like challenges." I laugh. His unbelieving stare cuts through me and pulverizes my confidence into crumbs. *How can he do that? This is part of the test, but what kind of a test is it?*

The smile that has firmly appeared on my lips becomes stiffer with every moment. I cannot lose, but I feel that I am losing.

"Challenges!" My potential boss is a sympathetic man around forty, with greyish hair and thick eyebrows. He nods. This interview is strange, and Lewis is even weirder. "Tell me who you are!" His eyes suddenly blink.

"I have been educated in..." I puff out my cheeks, feeling deceived. *I have already told him. Didn't he hear me?*

"No." He interrupts and sits closer. "I am not interested in your formal skills. Who are *you*, Maggie Kent?"'

Slowly, I take a breath. *How philosophical do I have to be? And what exactly do I need to say?*

"I want this job," I tell him, crossing my fingers. "This might amuse you, but my grandmother gave me the desire to become a salesperson. She sold flowers in the market. I often sat next to her and watched. She told me, 'A good sales process is not just an exchange of goods for money; it requires much more. You must have a discussion with every buyer—about the price of the bouquet, the weather, and when the land has to be ploughed up." Even then, I noticed that the buyers returned. Not only because of the good price, but because my grandmother was waiting for them, and remembered them. It was fascinating—every time the same people came to her and brought up new people with them. Then one day I realized that I also want to be a salesperson—that I want to change the sales world and help people!" I paused. "I want to be a part of this huge mission. I cannot even express how much I want *this* job!"

Ed is watching me. *Have I sold myself?*

"Great!" he grins, leaning back on the bench. "That is a very good answer! Thank you."

I grin, my courage increasing by leaps and bounds, and I am proud. "*Maggie*," in my mind I am tapping myself on the shoulder, "*you are making progress!*" I try to be serious, but already I am smiling, anticipating that the job will be mine. *Hold on—I am coming!*

The Phone Book

I am wearing my most beautiful high-heeled shoes and an elegant skirt suit that perfectly shows off my narrow shoulders, tanned skin and light hair color. I am going to work. Starting today, I am the junior salesperson in the technology company Tamm Solutions. They have developed the best customer management system (CRM) in the world, enabling companies to more effectively monitor their business, including creating calendars and invoicing in virtual environments. I go down the street and smile, convinced that this work is my destiny.

Ed, the Tamm sales manager, called me the day after the interview and offered me the job. And I, like every army private, was told that I could start to work right away. Tamm Solutions has a stylish office in the city center, sales training, business trips, excellent growth opportunities, an international team, a motivating salary and even bonuses from the sale of systems. Also, pretty challenging—working with clients, the managers of companies. Furthermore, the company provides a computer, a phone, paid transportation, health insurance, a gym membership, and a short work day on Fridays. I also assume that the work environment, which can be arranged to my taste, will have a wonderful view from the window, and coworkers from whom I can learn a lot. How could I say no to such a job?

The street is full of tall, modern glass buildings, and it is mainly the branches of foreign companies that are located here. Tamm is not an exception. I stop and enjoy the view, then march on.

My friends will be green with envy, especially Erica, my apartment buddy, who thinks that salespeople are annoying liars and cutthroats who live underground and whom you should avoid. "They are robots, most of whom do not even believe in the products they are selling," Erica declared me yesterday. "Be careful that they do not entice you into some unemotional sect that can be entered only by obscene communications network service advisors, and mattress salespeople who only know how to bother you with their unnecessary products." I know that Tamm is not like this, and when Erica understands how happy I am, she'll have to change her mind.

I hope that my mother will also change her mind. She always worries that if I follow my "ridiculous idea" about becoming a career salesperson, my reality will be earning only the minimum wage. I love my mother, her personality and patience, and her endless support for reaching my goals in life, but she thinks that salespeople stand behind the counter and sell tomatoes. Or flowers, in my grandmother's case. Mom thinks that this dream will lead me to a grocery store, or a kiosk, where I will squander my talent on long working hours. She'd rather see me as a lawyer or a doctor, or a programmer.

But I know and feel much more. Salespeople really do sell, but only few of them are selling excellently. They work with large entrepreneurs, receive huge bonuses, participate in significant conferences and run workshops. The media speaks about them, they are praised by their coworkers and every entrepreneur wants to have them on their team, but only some of them can afford these excellent salespeople. They have a three-bedroom penthouse apartment with a view of the city skyline, the latest *Audi* model, easy entrance to glitzy night parties, and the president is on their contact list.

I will also have it. I. Will.

I'll prove it! It's me. And this is not naivete of the young girl that sprouted in the countryside and is not acquainted with the real and dishonest world. I know a lot more about sales than some good city dwellers. I believe in my power and have inherited a love for technology from my dad, an engineer, and I have a big heart. I am an idealist and believe that everything happens exactly as it should. The world has no alternatives. I will build the world as it is appropriate for me.

I walk forward to the revolving glass door. Tamm Solutions is in a really beautiful new building, with dark glass everywhere. As I approach the revolving door, it turns. A man exits, and I disappear inside. Starting today, my life will get better.

***

A secretary awaits me in the lobby. She takes me to the company's offices, up the stairs to the second floor. The inside of Tamm Solutions looks elegant; the interior is designed in a Scandinavian style, with light wood furniture and art objects. I will like it here.

"Maggie," says Ed, coming towards me. "Nice to see you!"

"Hello," I nod to the chief.

"How are you?" he asks politely.

"Very good, thanks!"

"Great!" he points and addresses the secretary. "Sofia! Meet Maggie, our junior salesperson."

"Hi!" Sofia smiles, and I answer her greeting.

"What can I say? Welcome to Tamm Solutions! Your journey begins now. Keep your eyes open." Lewis laughs, it seems that today he's in a good mood.

My new boss kindly offers his services as a guide and proceeds to show me around the company. We go to the largest meeting room, located on the left side of the hallway and separated from the reception room by large, two-leaved glass doors.

"Pharaoh." I look in through the open door and read the inscription on the wall.

"Yes, each meeting room has a name. When a customer is coming, you can quickly reserve this room on the calendar. You can also book any other Tamm meeting room on the calendar," Ed reveals. We go down the hallway displaying various awards the company has won, and posters with encouraging slogans hanging on the walls. "Passion is the key" is one of them. I suspect that the goal of the posters is to cheer up the customers and employees and reading them I feel that I would like to get to work quickly.

"Also, on the left side is 'Vizier,' intended for smaller meetings and individual sessions. You will see it later; there is a meeting in there right now."

We come the furthest end of the building, where a small room with green walls, a table and two chairs are located. "Aquarium" is written on the wall.

"People call it CSC—the Call Suffering Center! You will spend most of your time here, calling customers."

THE RECEIVER IS NOT AN ENEMY

– "YEAH RIGHT..."

The receiver is not an enemy, I murmur, noticing the framed card on the windowsill. It shows a strange scene with an old-fashioned telephone receiver hanged in gallows. There's no shortage of imagination here, and I admire that.

After visiting the CSC, the kitchen and the cellar, we come to the rooms where the project managers and accounting department are located, surrounded by gray walls and decorative plants. I meet my coworkers, and I feel great. There is nothing nicer than a sense of belonging, and I am proud that now I am officially part of this company.

"In total, Tamm employs twenty-eight people, and eleven of them work here." We pass Ed's office and arrive in the sales team's room, which is located on the other side of the reception room. We have returned to the starting point, and my excitement has no limits any more. I have waited for the day when I will be able to fulfill my dreams, and now it has finally come!

The room is bright, with large windows and wall posters highlighted by the sun.

"A comfort zone is the most beautiful place—where nothing grows." It is the largest one, red with white letters and placed almost next to the entrance. Ed touches it significantly and forgets about me for a second. *What does it mean?* I wrinkle my nose—*doesn't Ed know that it looks very strange?* I look around. There is also a sofa, and a huge bookcase on the nearby wall. This is my reality! Fantastic! Ed says that including me, the sales department has grown to four people. I watch my new coworkers. There are two men and a woman who work together, shoulder-to-shoulder.

"Maggie, this is Ralph." The boss points to a meager, red-haired young man who sits in the left corner, at the window. "Ralph has been the top salesperson for the last two months! It is definitely worthwhile to learn from him."

"Hi," I wave. "Hi, everybody!"

The tour of the building ends at my table, located away from the others, next to the printer and the fire extinguisher. I am a little upset, because it means there will be noise—and where is my beautiful view from the window? I have been seated in the gloomiest corner of the room. I want to say something but change my mind.

"Decorate your work space as you choose. This is yours!" Ed points to the small table and the simple armchair next to it.

I am confused, and I feel isolated from the rest of team. How shall I conquer the heads of companies from such corner? Biting my tongue, I calm down. *It's nothing*, I admonish myself. *It might be the normal way they test new employees. I am welcome here; the computer and phone on my desk is the proof of that. Everything is prepared, ready for me to begin my work. I will prove myself, and then being seated at a better table will be only a matter of time.*

"Maggie," Lewis takes a book with a blue cover from the bookshelf, "when we are finished, go to the accounting room and sign the contract."

"Ok!"

"Then let's start working!" says the sales guru, as Ed has been called by other business people. He opens a book, the telephone directory. He rips out the first page and gives it to me. "Please, arrange meetings with directors of these companies."

"What?" I stretch out a hand to grab the page, but it slides back without even touching the page. This situation stuns me. *What? Right now? He can't be serious!* I collapse, as if waiting to be slapped. I sit up straighter, but unconsciously my shoulders are falling down. Already!

"Arrange meetings with the directors of those companies." Ed speaks impassively, and there is no trace of the decency and joy that were there a moment ago.

I swallow my saliva feverishly—now, the unconditional obedience phase begins. *This is my first task? It's nothing to worry about*, my ego is screaming in my ear. *How can I do that?* I am surprised and angry at the same time, and I hope it doesn't show on my face.

"Good!" I gather my enthusiasm and grab the page. My fears are banished. *Hold on— if you don't stay on the front line, you'll capitulate!* "I will let you know how I'm doing."

"Please do so!" The boss squeezes my hand. "Good luck!"

Ed goes out. He has given me one single task, but without any instructions. It's almost funny. *No training, and a job to do.* So suddenly! It's like a cold shower. *Elementary,* I encourage myself, *standard procedure! But I know nothing!* Despair starts to arise and waylays me like a wolf. *I have nothing. No knowledge. No training. Nothing. I have been thrown in the battlefield without a winning card in my pocket. I am the journeyman without a master or tools.* I look at the page from the telephone book, which includes some respectable American business giants, whose directors most probably hide behind their secretary and many assistants. *It's spooky.*

I start to read the page more carefully, and instinctively guess that this is a huge opportunity. While I am *trying* to get used to that idea, I look at my coworkers. Ralph is not interested in me anymore. I return to reading the page. *If I get these giants on my customer list, I will improve my career very quickly. I will fight with Ralph for huge customers from the beginning!* My courage triples and I do not care about the others.

Yes, it's true that I do not know how to make cold calls, but that is just a trifle— you just pick up the receiver and talk. As I know now, *the receiver is not my enemy.* I get up and sit down. Stand up. Sit down. And stand up. And sit down. *What do I need to get started?*

***

Before beginning my task, I decide to thoroughly research my coworkers here at Tamm Solutions. I open my notebook, which I specifically bought for my work as a salesperson and note the location of each of my coworkers in order to memorize the hierarchy here faster.

Ralph Meinard, I think, poking my finger at his picture. *Who are you?* Slightly peeking over at the top salesperson, I am trying to find out what skills I need to learn in order to win the sales battle. But I cannot see anything except his red hair, pale face and thin lips. I check his *LinkedIn* profile, and I have to admit that it is impressive. Besides working for Tamm, he has also been a sales manager for the largest IT corporation, and is a lecturer working at the University of New York. If I had studied there, he even could have been one of my teachers!

I need a friend like Ralph. I click on *"Connect"* to add him to my own network of contacts on *LinkedIn*. I get up to go to him for advice regarding a cold call but change my mind. Asking for help in the first hours of my new job would not be cool! *What would they think of me? What if Ralph tells Ed? No! I can't do that.* I sigh and quit the idea. *It's better to do it myself. I can do it without help! And how difficult could it be?*

***

Pharaohs is the pride of Tamm Solutions. A projector, a coffee machine and a whiteboard are placed near the glass table with metal legs and ten chairs with high backs, and there is a yucca in the corner—a plant that absorbs negative emotions arising from failed transactions. Everything in Pharaohs is governed by intelligent systems; even the blinds are opened and closed only by remote control. At the present, my attention is attracted by the painting with some ancient Egyptian motif of a pharaoh and one of his gods in the center. *That's why these rooms have such names.* I shrug my shoulders. The painting differs a lot from that of the ancient Egyptian times I have read about in history books, and I guess that this particular work of art is likely to be a modern artist's interpretation of the ancient world. Interesting.

I leave ancient Egypt in the past and sit down at the conference table. After being daunted by that unfortunate phone directory, ridiculing me on my very first day, I have regained my energy. Google has helped me, and the first discussion draft is ready.

It's a promising start. I can do it! Pushing the hair curl behind my ear, I grab the phone from the table and make a call. First on the list is a medium-sized company that is engaged in metal processing. One of the giants.

I am calling.

A TELEPHONE CALL SCRIPT

1. INTRODUCTION
   - WHO AM I?
2. THE OBJECTIVE
   - WHY DO I CALL?
   - DO I HAVE AN APPOINTMENT?
   (NO, BUT YOU NEED TAMM)
   - WHEN CAN WE MEET?
3. FAREWELL
   - THANK YOU

With each beep I feel my heartbeat accelerating. *What is going on?* No one is speaking to me yet, but by the third beep my heart is already thundering along like a jockey on a horse. *What should I say? Remember the plan. Remember! You can do it! "Hello, my name is Maggie and I want to talk to...."*

My heart is beating more and more rapidly. My mouth becomes dry. *Hello, my name is... It seems that my hair will turn grey on this call!* I tremble inside, and I am afraid that it might be noticeable in my voice. *Remember!* The fifth beep. The sixth.

Missed it. Missed it? Missed it! My excitement bursts like a soap bubble, and my heart rate slows down as if by magic. *Missed it!* I'm laughing in my thoughts. The eighth beep. *They missed my call!*

I cut the connection and put the phone back down on the table. My hands are still trembling a bit, and my head and stomach start to hurt. It seems that I have lost my sense of balance. The painting on the wall seems bizarre and meaningless. For a second, I forget who I am and what I am doing in Tamm Solutions. Grabbing my head in my hands, I count to ten. I am a little distraught. They missed my call. It's not my fault, is it? I did my job. I have got to get in some fresh air, relax and feel my freedom.

My mood is changing at lightning speed—now I am disappointed. Nobody answers me. After all the excitement, the time spent collecting information and preparing for the call, nothing happened. It cannot be that I no one will answer me! I feel that destiny has fooled me and hides as from a small child. I puff out my cheeks and continue with the next phone number. It is another metal processing company.

Calling. Beep. Two beeps. My fingers tremble, and again my throat dries. Third beep. *Why does my body resist?*

"Metals LLC, hello?" There is a voice from other end of the handset, and my brain starts to boil.

"Good afternoon!"

"Good afternoon."

"I want to talk to Oliver Fallon." *I am direct and unbreakable,* I think, and it makes me a bit more courageous. *I'm talking.* Indeed, I am talking.

"He is not available right now. How may I help you?"

"I'm Maggie, from Tamm Solutions. We are a company that develops business management tools. Since you are one of the leading companies in the industry, we want to offer you a tool that will improve your business!" I speak very quickly. My mind is like a burner attached to dynamite, only one minute away from a tragedy, and I am afraid that due to my internal panic I'll forget what I need to say.

"We don't accept offers over the phone. It doesn't work that way." The secretary's voice becomes firmer.

Failure. Can it be? My head droops down. *I could lose this deal. How can I save it?* I'm unable to think, and words sink in my mouth like a log in a swamp.

"E-mail us your offer and we will evaluate it. If we are interested, we'll get back to you," she tells me.

"How soon do you usually reply?" My whole body feels heavy. *What's happening to me?*

"As I said, if it interests us, we will respond. You can find our e-mail address on our website."

'Thank you," I wheeze. I have a headache; it feels as if I am on a carousel, being pelted with words that I do not understand. "Goodbye."

"Goodbye!"

There are no sounds in the telephone receiver, only inexplicable silence. I put the phone on the table and stare blankly into the corner of the Pharaohs room. I pick at the hem of my skirt and look at the painting again. I began to laugh, thus dispersing the void that fills my soul.

Laughter surrounds each cell, and I put my hand to my mouth to slow down my overflowing emotions. *My first cold call is over, and I'm still alive! Crazy! What do you say, Maggie? What do you say, pharaoh?*

My adrenaline stabilizes, and I make another call. One time. Two times. Three times. Within an hour, I make seven calls, and after each of them drag I myself out of a psychological decline. My tongue disobeys, and my wisdom stutters, but I am fulfilling my assigned responsibilities. I do not believe that I will not succeed. That can't happen. My confidence declines, plummets, hits rock bottom, and then I renew my forces and stand on the starting line again.

After the last call my forehead falls against the table and my hand slips off. *That's enough for today.* I relax for a few minutes and then go back to my office. I've done a good job. My results are four refusals, two missed calls, and one invitation to e-mail the company. At least that's something to surpass in the future. I can still call some of the larger companies on Ed's list, and

THE HELL FOR CALLS

that motivates me. I still have a little time.
Quite a bit, actually.

***

After lunch I see Ralph in the courtyard
behind the building. He is sitting on a
plastic chair with his legs crossed, wearing
sunglasses, and looking extremely
mysterious. This is my opportunity to get
closer to one of my coworkers, so I sit
down beside him. My look stops at the
large black glass windows of the building.
What a view from the courtyard. I
shudder.

"How did you manage with the phone
directory?" I ask, after the first welcoming
phrases and questions

"Okay." Ralph is a little tense and reserved.

"I didn't expect that to happen! I have never had made cold calls. It's frightening," I murmur. "What do you suggest?"

Ralph looks at me, sniffing his nose. I don't like it when I can't see his eyes.

"You didn't call anyone today?"

"I called!"

"Then you can't say that you haven't made cold calls." Ralph laughs and sinks back in the chair. *It's as if he doesn't care about anything. How can Ralph McCarren can be the best salesperson?* "What do you want, Maggie?"

"I want to do my job! I thought you could help me," I say.

"Well, why did you put on this costume?"

"What?" My voice falters. *What do my clothes have to do with cold calls?*

"Why are you wearing that?"

"It's required by business etiquette."

"What business, Maggie?" Ralph looks over me from head to toe and smiles cunningly. When I do not answer, my coworker hisses and his smile fades. He removes his sunglasses and leans closer— and his look is full of harshness. "I've seen other people like you! You arrive aiming to get *my* chair. With a sense of vanity, as if it is self-evident that you deserve everything, for free! But it's not that way, Maggie! Have you ever looked in the mirror and asked yourself, 'what is a *genuine* salesperson?'"

It feels as if someone has hit me in the chest. Ralph's attitude leaves me dumbfounded. *What? I'm a fighter, not a lounger!* He makes me seem less of an adult, and I do not intend to tolerate that! I pout and get up. *I won't stay here any longer. I do not want anything from Ralph! Why did I send him a contact request on LinkedIn?*

"If you don't play by the right rules, you will not survive here." He puts on the sunglasses. "If you don't play your cards right, you will lose all the money you paid for your costume, just trying to land the large customers."

What does he know?

"Don't get sick with The Pharaoh's Curse. Being at the top is not a gift, if you have no mouth, eyes and ears—and a bit of understanding!"

What are you mumbling about? Idiot! Mr. Intolerable! Fine—Ralph will hear about me! Let's see who will be the better salesperson next month!

I realize that none of salespeople will help
me, and that I have to fight for my status
in society by myself. There is no room for
friendship. I have to learn alone, and prove
that by choosing me, Ed has not made a
mistake. I shall be the victor and crash my
opponents. I am not going to give up.

Never.

Profile Case

The next day starts with a daily meeting, in which my coworkers tell about the work they accomplished the previous day and the team's progress is evaluated. In addition to me, Ed, Ralph and two other salespeople attend the meeting. I sit down on a chair next to Ralph and wait to see what will happen.

"Hello, *Tamms*! What's new?" Ed sits down at the table, at the short end.

"Oil prices have decreased on the stock exchange!" exclaims Carl, the guy with dark hair and a pronounced chin.

"Then you will probably not buy a new car," Ralph laughs.

"I guess not!" responds Carl.

"Great! Maggie, how do you feel?" asks Ed.

"Perfect!" I grin.

"Welcome to the first meeting! I hope that you succeeded yesterday," says the chief. "By the way, we have a tradition that any coworker who delays a meeting brings doughnuts for the whole team the next day!"

I blink my eyes.

"Everyone arrived on time today. That's just for the information for the future. Discipline is highly appreciated here," he continues. "Now let's go through what we're working on. I will begin with myself. I have a discussion with *Silence International*. They are ready to take our *premium* offer and the large system implementation program. Today we will correct some nuances of the contract, and then it will be ready for signing!"

Ed is a giant. Monumental. He speaks as if the business arrangement would be most elementary work on the planet. He has no hesitation, no lack of belief his own forces. I want to be like him, self-confident to the very end.

"What they did not like in the contract?" Anna, a girl with short brown hair and cheek dimples, asks. She was hired half a year before me, and currently works with the VIP clients.

"The amount of time it will take to implement the program in their company. It is a trifle; it will be handled quickly. Yes...I have just booked the dates with *Femmet* Company and *Carley Motors*. We'll see the amount that we have to talk about. Maggie," he focuses on me again, "We usually call the meeting 'a date.' For us it symbolizes the beginning of building a relationship with the client, a time when it is important to develop mutual sympathies. You will have to be charming!"

I smile and nod. *"Date" is a peculiar term!*

"That is all for me. Anna, will you continue?"

Anna, and later Carl, tell about their achievements. Yesterday both of them have arranged two dates each, in addition to Anna's conversation with a potential customer turning into a very profitable transaction. The quick accomplishments of my coworkers make me think. *What will I tell them tomorrow? How many rejections I've received?* That would not improve my reputation. Ed and Ralph give advice on how to deal with unwanted customers, but I don't hear them anymore. They are so good at sales. But I have that *idiotic* page! *They'll laugh at me,* I think, and look at the bookshelf.

"Maggie?" Ed addresses me.

"Yes?" I straighten my back.

"What are your thoughts about your work yesterday?"

"My thoughts?" my cheeks flame. *Mine? What? Why? I'm not talking today. I just listen. I haven't prepared anything! No!* "Mine? Mmm ... I made a number of cold calls yesterday. And mmm ... I set up a negotiation script."

Run, Maggie, catch your hand and run away.
I am speechless. I have nothing to say. Why didn't anybody tell me that I have to speak in this meeting? In *this particular meeting*? After one working day?

"Great! Will you share it? Is there anything that doesn't work?"

What kind of a question is that? My fingers do not obey me and remembering seems like endless torture. *That's it. I failed.* How can I compete with the transactions the others have concluded? I take a breath and close my eyes. There should be the way out.

"I'm not sure what to do—how to get past the secretary."

'Try to give a compliment," Ralph suggests. "Sometimes it works!"

Ralph smiles and enjoys my failure. I seems that I will sink in his pride. Compliment? Compliment what?

"Yes, that's a good idea! You can check whether the company has recently received an award. Flattery may be useful," Ed and Ralph preen. I flatten myself against the back of my chair.

"Anything else?"

Dismissively, I shake my head. I have nothing. I am shocked.

"Ralph?"

Ralph describes his previous day like it happened in a poem, being authoritative and attainable. Like Lewis. It hurts me. *Why can't I get results like that?* I must have dazed Ed somehow. What *did I say, and why can't I repeat it?*

"Super, team! Is that all? No more announcements?" Lewis claps his hands. "Then let's get to work! And remember, salespeople never sleep. Let's meet tomorrow."

Ed gets up and leaves the room, without even looking at me. He is so powerful. Ralph looks back at the boss. *He* would like to be so powerful. Meanwhile, I have to live with public humiliation. I sneeze and get back to work. My time will come too!

***

"No, thank you, we are not interested in this kind of offer," says the woman who answered the telephone, interrupting me in mid-sentence before I managed to introduce myself properly. Why? I drop the receiver and hiss. It seems that even the change of room is not helping me. After Ed's admonition not to use *Pharaohs* for cold calls, today I am working in *Aquarium*, and this room gradually makes me feel smaller. I cannot stand it. I realize why *Aquarium* is called the call suffering center. *Failure again.*

The second working day has turned out to be like fearful guillotine around the neck, ready to cut off my head at the first opportunity. My excitement has gone, and I am staring at the phone that has become my biggest torturer. Does anybody else hate something as much as I hate the telephone right now? *The receiver is not an enemy.* I look at the card on the windowsill and mumble that someone should reassess the status of this non-enemy. And I hate those wretched secretaries, who think that they do work that is useful to society. Nonsense! You think I'm laughing? They do not know how to think! Without pressing the call button, I want the secretary who answers my call to choke on her lunch. How can I compliment them later?

Make up your mind, I reprimand myself. *Maggie, get on with it*! I must not ask Ralph and Ed for mercy in order to get my work done. No, I will not give them such an honor. None of them.

My thoughts are disturbed by the knock at the door, and I look across the room to see Ed enter. Today, together with Anna, he has concluded the biggest deal in the history of Tamm Solutions and is currently at the zenith of his fame. Their triumph was highlighted by the Tamm sales bell, which is rung each time when a new deal has been concluded. The bell is located in the third row of bookshelf and is major messenger of victory here. Mr. Unbearable looked self-satisfied, and I can bet that ringing sound fed his hypocrisy. I also want to ring the bell. I want to be in Ralph's place.

"Hello! How are you?" Ed sits down in front of me.

"Good!" I give a laborious smile.

"Can I help you?"

Can you release me from this task and finally allow me to participate in the growth of Tamm? I think.

"How many dates have you arranged for next week?" Ed asks. I shudder. Yes, he is interested only in this.

"None yet. A couple are in process," I tell him, lowering my eyes. I am ashamed of my results.

"Maggie, you're a human. It is normal to be afraid."

What? I am not afraid. How do you know? I stare at Ed, who looks at me almost like father, and it gives me a dose of self-confidence. *He knows. Of course!*

"I cannot get it," I admit, feeling weak, like an animal that has lost its defenses. "Cold calls..."

"It is part of your job," says Lewis. "You cannot run away from them."

"I know!"

"But you can deal with them?"

Deal? I'm finished!

"Maggie!" Ed sighs. "Please, give me the sheet of paper?"

I nod and pull out one sheet from my notebook. Ed grabs a pen and writes my name in the center of sheet.

"That's you!" he points. "Not only your name. All of you. And all of the emotions characterizing you! However, only when you start to control your emotions will you be able to deal with current difficulties. Maggie, concentrate! You are not here because of my sadistic tendencies, or because I like to watch how you suffer. You're in *Tamm* because I want you to be the part of our team! Talk to yourself and realize what is going on. What is bothering you?"

"Fear! I'm afraid!"

"Super!"

Oh, really? I do not understand what's so good about it!

"You thought that you would always live in your comfort zone? There's a reason why the poster devoted to the comfort zone is located in the sales office. Remember? Nothing grows there! In addition, the comfort zone is not only boring, but also degrading! Fear, Maggie, indicates that you knowingly—or perhaps unconsciously—fight to get away from your comfort zone." Ed draws an arrow out from my name and writes *Fear*. "Are you the Maggie who runs away? Who doesn't take risks? Who doesn't take chances? Are you a person who has such a huge self-defense mechanism that you only want to be only in places where nothing endangers you?"

I shrug my shoulders. I've proved that I can postpone working quite successfully. In order to protect myself, I use my common sense. I check what can be expected on the other end of the telephone receiver. I reassure myself. I do not make calls until I have ascertained the name of the secretary, manager or sales manager, and seen their *Facebook* and *LinkedIn* profiles. True, I wait until everything has been checked. The green Call button paralyses me, and I do not want to let that into my life. And then I postpone making calls, hoping that sending e-mails out first will be my panacea. Is that fear?

"Maggie, are you with me?"

"Yes! I'm here!" I give Ed a frail smile.

"Do you know the bitter truth? Salespeople also are afraid! The difference is, are you ready to defeat your fear?" He pauses. "I need something else from you." Ed draws another arrow from my name and writes *Courage*. "I'm looking for salespeople who have ambitions! Those who take risks, are not afraid, and are endowed with transcendental faith in themselves. Who speak, listen and see! The ones who were afraid but are afraid no longer! Who would make it a daily ritual to come to the comfort zone poster in the salespeople's room, and tell themselves "I will work, I will not tolerate failure, and will I not allow fear to defeat me!"

I knit my eyebrows together. *Is that why he touched the poster?*

FEAR ← MAGGIE → COURAGE

"Maggie, the Tamm sales team is superstitious," states my boss.

I want to be like that. Courageous. Strong. I like this vison of who Maggie could be! Is it her who brought each dream that exists in my head? I want to fight! I want to be special Maggie, who is not ashamed of herself and takes confident steps. It is my ideal. I have to shine! There is no other choice!

"You must get rid of assumptions about what to do and how you have to act. Forget everything you expect from this job, because only then will you become a salesperson!"

What is he talking about?

"Do you know what an assumption is? It is your thoughts about everything that is happening around you. Your judgments about what a salesperson is, what the customer is, and who are you. And there will be moments when you will have a lot of negative assumptions, and they will be followed by disappointment, disbelief in yourself and this profession. Replace them with good assumptions! Trust in courage, not fear!"

Ed's words inspire me, and I want to say that already I am proud to be here. I promise to improve myself. To eliminate things that distract me from success. To always remember whether I want to be afraid or brave. I was afraid, but that is in the past now.

"To help you, tomorrow I have arranged for you to do a call session with Ralph."

Inwardly, I collapse. *Why does it have to be Ralph? Ralph is a monster. He does not know how to talk and is rude. I will not work with such person! No.*

"Ralph is a fantastic professional," adds the boss. "Learn from him while you can."

Learn from him? Mr. Unbearable does not let anyone close to him, so how can I learn? After such an inspiring speech, Ed drops me into hopelessness again. *He does not understand that I cannot communicate with Ralph McCarren.*

***

I can do it.

Opening the notebook, between the pages I find the portrait of Maggie drawn by Ed. I borrow Scotch tape and scissors from my coworkers and stick the drawing on the wall. It will be my lighthouse when I feel sad. *My profile cases. Do not be afraid.* I feel a tap on my shoulder.

"Maggie?" My excitement is ruined by Ralph. I wrinkle my nose. "It's ten o'clock! Let's go!"

I grab my notebook, pen and phone and run after him. The competition has begun!

"Do you know why we will start to call now?" he asks, upon entering *Aquarium,* which suddenly looks even narrower. Is claustrophobia like that, when you are in the same room with an unwelcome person?

"No." I overcome my thoughts and harden my face. *Focus!*

"The hours from 10:00 a.m. till 4:00 p.m. are the best for calling— the so-called 'prime time!" Try to arrange your day according to this principle," says Mr. Unbearable, putting his hands on the table.

"Thanks for the advice!"

He does not sit down. Do I also have to stand?

"Can you show me your list?"

I give the page from the phone directory to Ralph, and he reads the names of the companies and their phone numbers.

"It's clear these are all metalworking companies." He looks at his watch, "From now until lunch we should deal with the third part of this list. How much of them have you called?"

I do not answer, and just put in front of him the current call statistics and wait for a reprimand.

"You've studied all this?" Ralph's attention is attracted by my detailed records about the companies; they also include data on annual reports and feedback from forums and social media.

"Yup!"

"Excellent, Maggie! I did not know that you gathered so much information." He blinks. *Was that a compliment?* "I can see how long you postponed calling! Excellent information, but rather useless."

I laugh. Ralph gave me a compliment, then took it away again. He is insulting, but funny.

"Please, sit down. Let's get started. Let's make it a game, like table tennis. I will make the first call, and you listen and write down notes about my conversation. Then you call, and I will listen and write notes about your conversation. Deal?"

No, it is not okay! I have to make cold calls in front of Ralph? Why?

"Deal?" he asks again.

I was afraid, but I am no longer afraid. Sigh. "Why not?"

"You have the name for this! Great!" Ralph picks up the phone, looks at the name of the company and calls. Without any pause. *Immediately. As if he was calling a friend about going to a basketball game in the evening.* I know that he's showing off, but still, he manages to convince me. Even without starting a conversation, Mr. Unbearable exudes invincible confidence without any fear of what's coming.

I turn the notebook toward me and begin to write notes. *What could I comment on? Maybe the fact that he is a conceited scoundrel? It would fit!*

"Hello, Dolet Steel!" a female voice answer. The speaker is turned on, so I can hear too.

"Hello." Ralph greets her and becomes silent.

The silence lasts for one second, until she asks, "Hello, how can I help you?"

"I am calling to arrange a meeting with John Stephens. Please, connect me!" Ralph says it in such a tone that it is as if it were an undisputed fact that John wanted the meeting.

"One moment." The secretary is suspicious, and I hear the clatter of computer keys in the background. "How do I introduce you?"

"Ralph from Tamm Solutions." Mr. Unbearable still talks in a convincing and authoritative voice.

"Connecting," mutters the secretary, and I roll my eyes. *How did he do that?*

"*Hello*?" answers John Stephens. *Incredible!*

"Hello, I'm Ralph from Tamm Solutions!"

Ralph pauses, and the prospective client has no choice but to continue to talk.

"Hello, what kind of meeting are we talking about?"

"I propose to meet and discuss the improvement of your sales team's efficiency. We have already helped to achieve excellent sales results in several other companies in your industry, and I am convinced that Dolet Steel can also be a winner! Would you have half an hour on Monday at eleven in the morning or on Tuesday at four o'clock for the meeting with me? I would be happy to come to your office." Ralph is precise, and in a calm voice he quotes the words that would fit in a promotional flyer. My thoughts are flying; I want to connect to Ralph's uniqueness and surpass it. I repeat his words to myself, so not to forget them.

"Interesting! Let me check my calendar...I will have time for a conversation with you on Tuesday."

'Then we have agreed to meet on Tuesday at four o'clock in your office at 18 54th Street," Mr. Unbearable repeats, and Stephens confirms it. "See you then and have a successful week!"

"See you!"

Ralph finishes the conversation, records the date in my notebook, and gives me the phone.

"Boom!" He reinforces his ego, and my hand freezes in the air. I feel awkward, and hope that during the next few seconds I will fall through the floor. Even if I do, I know that I will look like a nonentity to Ralph.

"What can you say about my conversation?"

"It was concise. And convincing."

Ralph sits and grins, as if my answer seems frivolous and not informative to him. What else could I tell him? What? Think! What did he say? *Ralph did not say anything about Tamm to the secretary*, I remember. Small memory threads appear in my brain. *He just asked to be connected to Stephens, in a convincing tone of voice.* Why didn't the secretary question Ralph, and torture him as they usually do with me? *Then Ralph told the customer that he will help to improve sales, and Stephens agreed to meet him.* I continue to delve into the conversation of my coworker. *And that's it?*

"Now you," Ralph murmurs.

I screw up my face. *I do not want to make a call.* My fear returns with devastating force. It is here; it does not disappear. *Mr. Unbearable is pressuring me, and I do not like it. What did he say? I do not remember anything! I can't do it. I am not able to do it. Why do I have to make cold calls if Ralph is so good at it? Don't be a growler!* Fighting my thoughts, I try to put my fear away. Please!

"With so much speed we won't be finished until the evening," my coworker laughs.

Idiot!

Dialing the next number, I feel bad. What was it that Ralph did? I want to stand up, but my body holds me.

"Hello!" I'm surprised by a man's voice. *"Hello?"*

"Hello, my name is Maggie," I say, holding Ralph's conversation in my memory. Suddenly it is so dim. "May I disturb you for a while?"

"About what?"

Yes, about what? What am I supposed to say? Ralph does not look at me, he just writes down his comments. He has so many of them! Why? I am more interested in the redheaded heartless person and his notes, not the guy secretary.

"Hello?"

Oh, where is my telephone call script?

"I am Maggie, and I represent the technology company Tamm Solutions, who develop client management systems. Can I talk to Peter Sherman?" I am businesslike, but even my tongue trembles and my hands are sweaty from excitement.

"We already have a customer management system!" the secretary sneers, and I hear it. "I doubt that we will change our existing system to yours!"

Am I the only one who thinks that the secretary says too much? How should I react?

"I appreciate your answer! It would be good to arrange a meeting in order to verify whether we can offer you something better."

The secretary falls silent. *What should I do?* I stare at Ralph, who does not give me any advice.

"I am connecting you now."

Oh, the thrill of emotion!

"*Hello*?" Sherman growls in the receiver.

I try to remember what Ralph did. *Improve sales. Make an appointment.*

"Hello, I'm Maggie from Tamm Solutions," I say, breathing into the receiver. I fidget in the chair in order to work off the anxiety. "I want to arrange a meeting with you about how to improve your sales results. Our company has developed a CRM system, and I can show you how it works!"

I don't like the words I have spoken, but at least I am talking. It will be enough.

"*What do you have*?" Sherman growls in an even lower tone.

"We have a calendar, invoicing, data storage..." in midstream, Ralph makes the cutthroat sign, telling me to stop talking about it. What should I say? "I'll see you in your office, and I will show... show you how the system works! Will you be available on Friday at 9 o'clock?"

"Let me check my schedule. Yes, I can see you then."

"Great!" I exclaim happily. "See you on Friday at 9 o'clock in your office at 50 49th Street!"

Sherman agrees.

"Goodbye!" I say, and hang up, blankly blinking my eyes. *Do I have a date?* Mr. Unbearable has screwed up his face. *He does not believe in my success?* I get up and sit down again.

"Maggie?"

I am all tensed up. I have such contradicting feelings that I cannot move, nor speak. *Should I be happy? Cry? What is going on?*

"What?"

"Ralph—I have a date!"

"That was the most terrible conversation that has ever led to a date. Congratulations!" my coworker says.

I jump up, raising my fists over my head. *I do not care. I will have a date! Yes*! I forget about the rest of the world, and joy surrounds me. The rest can wait—Ralph's comments about the accuracy of my conversation and my words. *I have to enjoy this moment. I would like this feeling to follow me. Always. Everywhere. Because it's my feeling. My dream is starting to come true. I am not afraid! Forward! Only forward!*

Mr. Customer

I am dressed in a black suit, ready to dazzle both Peter Sherman and Ralph, who has been sent by Ed Lewis to assist me. *Today I am fearless and able to meet anybody, regardless of their position, wealth and importance. Today I'll be the star of Tamm Solutions.*

While waiting for Ralph in Pharaohs, I repeat the story about Tamm. I know the company's history, the product features, the price list, and how the software can improve the customer's work.

"Hello, my name is Maggie." I extend my hand to nobody, just imagining the appointment. "Pleased to meet you! I am excited to show you Tamm Solutions!"

I walk around the room, since I have observed Ralph doing that. I imitate him. I have discovered that walking removes my anxiety and helps me to organize my thoughts. It is very helpful.

"Compliment!" I look in my notebook and slap my forehead. Giving a compliment is the first thing I must do.
"Congratulations, Mr. Sherman, on your company's newly acquired investment! Best wishes for further growth."

The phone rings, and I jump up.

"Hi, Ralph, I am waiting for you!" I am smiling. I cannot remember myself smiling at him recently.

"Hey, Maggie, something has come up, and I will not be able to accompany you to talk with Sherman."

"What?" My peace evaporates. "Why?"

"I'm sorry, I have to go to my daughter's kindergarten."

I get sour. *Since when does Ralph have a child?* I do not know what angers me more, the fact that he is leaving me or the fact that I can be left alone. "I understand," I tell him.

"Don't worry!" Ralph laughs. My fear returns. *No! Go away!* "You know everything, right? Are you ready?"

"Yes, Ralph, for sure! Go to your daughter. I will handle this."

"Ok, good. The main thing is to find out and understand what they need."

"Ok. Good luck!"

I hang up and sit down. Suddenly, I'm freezing. I want to wrap myself up in a blanket and hide from the world. I ignore the fear and stand up. *This is my chance!* I smooth out my skirt and straighten my jacket. I want to be proud of myself!

Go! I know everything. Everything! When it is difficult, I will have a chance to improvise. I will smile in order to create a good impression. I will explain why the software can help the company, because it is my duty. I will educate! I will not be ordinary, but special, and I will exude magic! I will be professional till the end!

***

I arrive on time at the office of my prospective client. On my way up to the fifth floor, I realize that I have no worries. *Hello, my name is Maggie.* I repeat the words for the hundredth time. For some reason, I want to enjoy this!

The secretary announces that Peter Sherman will not be able to participate, but I will meet the co-owner of the company, Raymond Vincent. Ok, good! He accompanies me to the meeting room, which—as befits the co-owner—is equipped with a massive working table and an eight-seat conference table. The bookcase is substantial and anciently brown, laden with books, and the walls display certificates of recognition. He's a big fish!

Vincent gets up from the chair and comes towards me. He's about 50 years old, a corpulent man with a serious face, and slightly grubby but businesslike clothing. After introducing ourselves we sit down at the far end of the conference table. I take out the notebook from my bag, open it to new page and begin the conversation without any worries.

"It is a great pleasure to meet you. Believe me, Tamm Solutions is the best choice for your company. Our software will solve your problems!"

"Please tell me what you can offer us. Then we will see if we are interested," replies Vincent. I hesitate for a moment. *Everything is going according to plan*; my courage tells me. "Very well," I agree. *Concentrate! Shine! Oh no—I forgot about the compliment! Never mind, it will be fine without it.*

"Tamm Solutions offers you our advanced CRM system, which is currently available in the market. Last year we won the award for the best business-technology oriented company in North America, and we have received wide publicity in the international media, including in *TechCrunch*. *TechCrunch* is one of the leading technology news media companies in the world." I outline our achievements, and continue with the description of our CRM's functions, emphasizing its unique algorithms and user experience that enables customers to review their projects, invoices and suppliers easily, as well as to keep up with the progress of their teams.

"Which functions work, normally?" my prospective customer asks, tapping his finger tips on the table.

"All our functions work *normally*" I say. "I would say, even more than normally!"

I proudly present the message board feature. It is the latest achievement of the Tamm programmers. This feature allows team members to publish information not related to the work, including events which may cause them to be absent from work for a certain period of time.

"If employee X is going to a wedding and will not be at work for two days, it will appear on the left side of the message board system, and the other employees see it. In addition, by entering specific dates in the message board, the calendar of that particular employee is blocked for those days, and if other coworkers want to include that employee in a meeting, the system will offer other dates."

Vincent seems interested. *I hit the top ten. Perfect!*

"Yes, this feature is the most recent contribution of Tamm Solutions. And, it is also included during the test period!"

Vincent takes his phone out of his jacket pocket, stands up and walks a few feet towards the door. *Will we have a deal? Incredible! My first deal in the first week!* My heart beats twice as fast. *What can I say now?* I have not planned it out!

"Hi!" my new acquisition says into his cell phone. "Let's go and have lunch!"

My joy melts, and suddenly I sweat as if I had run a marathon. *What is Vincent doing? I misheard, right?* Putting the phone back in his pocket, he turns to me.

"You can find your own way out." Vincent disappears from my sight, without even saying goodbye.

I am sitting with my notebook open, blinking my eyes. I am crushed. Courageous Maggie, for whom nothing was difficult, has gone up against impudent Vincent, and he left me empty-handed. His negligence stabs in my soul, leaving permanent scars. What went wrong? I bite my tongue to try and stop myself from crying, but the refusal hurts so much that I cannot hold back all my tears.

I've been betrayed. *Why did Sherman and Vincent invite me to come if they did not want to buy anything? I was interesting for a couple of minutes, and when it started to become boring, he got rid of me. Rudely.* I take my belongings and leave. I have no reason to be here anymore.

***

Upon returning to the office, my
indignation has grown. I've lost so much
time! So much! I will put Vincent on the
black list and take care that he gets the
worst version of the software if he ever
thinks it over and decides to cooperate
with us. Ralph catches me at the door to
the sales room.

"Maggie, how it was?"

"It was humiliating," I mumble.

"What? What happened?"

"First of all, I did not speak with Sherman
but the co-owner, Vincent! Second, he's an

idiot! In the middle of the date, he just got up and went to lunch—without any explanation! He insulted and had fun at my expense! Filled his free minutes!"

Ralph steps away, a little ashamed.

"I'm sorry that I left you alone."

'That's all right."

"It seems that you've just met Mr. Customer."

Who?

"These are clients who really do not need anything. They like to listen what you are trying to sell, but from the beginning they have no desire to buy anything. This kind of client exists. They just exist! Next time it will definitely be better!" My coworker smiles. "By the way, what have you learned?"

"A refusal sometimes hurts..."

"What questions did you ask?"

"I didn't ask anything! He threw me out before I managed to ask anything!"

"What did he say about their needs?"

"Nothing!"

"What did you do then?" Ralph is looking significantly changed, and the eyes that were full of pity are full of derision again. *What? Why?* My fears awaken and replace my sense of guilt. *What? Why?*

"I told him about Tamm. The product! Features!" I mumble quietly. Fear. The derision coming silently from Mr. Unbearable presses me like an insect, and I flatten even more.

"And you did not know what he needs?"

"Ralph ..."

Why am I the scoundrel now, not Vincent?

"Nobody conducts the meeting that way! It's as if you just tried sell the Eiffel Tower over the phone!"

"What?"

"Customers are not interested in functions! How well they work and how beautiful they look—nonsense! Imagine that the salesperson who sells the Eiffel Tower comes to you, and tells you how much it weighs, in which colors it is available, what material it is made of, and how you can use it, even if you are hearing about it for the first time. How can you be interested if you do not have any idea how it can help you? The salesperson does not even know whether you need it! Why do you think that Vincent would need Tamm if you present it this way?"

My coworker crashes another boulder on my soul.

"Never speak about the product if you do not know what the customer's problem is!"

"If you had not left me alone, I might have known that!" I say, and immediately regret it. But I have so much anger towards Vincent and so much discouragement from Ralph that I must build walls to protect myself.

"Maggie…" Ed addresses me from behind my back, and I step aside, like a convicted person driven into a corner. *Where is my joy? I was able to arrange a date with anyone, right?*

"Yes?"

"In two hours, I will meet you in Vizier for a one-to-one session."

What is that? What is going on? A one-to-one session? I look at Ralph, who has already sat down at his desk, and sigh. I've been abandoned. *I'm alone. Again. Just because I "tried to sell Eiffel Tower on the phone" at the meeting with Vincent.*

"Please, prepare what you have done this week. We shall make decisions about future cases." The boss does not notice my extreme discouragement.

"Yes," I agree humbly, like a small puppy, and put away any hopes of winning a dispute with Mr. Unbearable. In this battle, I lie down my weapons.

***

I look at the calendar, and for a moment I cannot believe it. "One to one session" is marked there in black and white.

Why did I not see that? I could not have missed it! I collapse. *Why do I have the feeling that everything is a game that tests my abilities?* No! I doubt they would spend time on that. I need to think. *Why am I stuck in a nightmare? I am afraid. It hurts. Fear. Courage. Is there a way out?*

Standard Requirement

This tension exhausts me. Everybody needs something. Ralph wants to have a full-fledged coworker. Ed needs cold calls, a phone directory and a one-to-one session. I also need something, but it seems that my dream job has turned into a valley of suffering. I am giving more than I am getting, and that's not fair. *What can I do, in general?* I look in the profile case and concentrate. *What else can I do?*

Always remember who you are. I write it on the sticker and stick to the profile case. *Who am I?* I remember the market, my grandmother, the flowers, the mission of a salesperson, and my ambition to become a professional in the craft. *That's me! Everything was so easy then. What do I have to admit now? The fact that it is difficult? Or the fact that Tamm is not the right place for me? Do I really divide into two opposites that deter me from success?* But I know that's not just black or white; there is also orange. There are so many colors that make up the human world, while mine consists of only two—fear and courage. *Why? Is it because Ed thinks that something else would be difficult for me?*

I Google to check what to expect from a one-to-one session, and at least from what

I read, I make up my mind that this meeting will change my situation in Tamm. It sounds scary, and I do not know if I am ready for it, either physically or morally. I raise my head and look at my coworkers. *Who I could ask about one-to-one sessions, and whether Ed tortures everybody and analyzes where the wisdom or—on the contrary—where their stupidity has been? Should I ask Ralph? No, after his betrayal and the accusations he expressed this morning, I do not want to sit with him, not even at a table at lunch.* My other coworkers also look too busy with their own issues. *Another time.*

I still have an hour. I shall prepare. What questions could he ask about my progress?

How was the last week? How do you evaluate your work?

I am learning, I will say. I go ahead. *This week I managed to*...how many calls I have made? I make a list and realize how chaotic it is; I have not processed the information, and it looks like a huge sheet with characters written on it. *Maggie, your organization is phenomenal!* I wrinkle my nose, but almost immediately I find the solution. Quietly, I laugh and start to implement my plan. I take a piece of cardboard and cut it in several small cards. After dividing them into five parts, I write the names of the companies I work with on them.

CONCLUDED | DEALS A DATE | REFUSALS | INTEREST | REMINDER

Great! I've organized 80 companies from the phone directory, and finally I can see what I've done this week. No, I have no deals yet, but each day I make more and more cold calls, despite the fact that I don't like them. Besides, I have also had the first meeting, which—although it did not end with the conclusion of a deal—showed that "Mr. Customers" exist. *Very well.* I stroke my pride. *The summary of my first week is quite positive.* The card system encourages me, and I do not feel sad any more. I order the courageous Maggie to stick those emotions. *Do not let them get away! Never!*

I return to the evaluation of my progress. *What else could be on Ed's list of questions?*

What plans do you have for the next week?

To continue the work I have begun, I will answer confidently, *I will work hard and fight to fulfill my potential.* There will be calls, dates, learning, and I will finish calling the companies on the phone directory page. I will have only positive assumptions, and courage. Smile blossoms on my face. I like working at Tamm, and I just started to pick up speed!

***

The sun shines in Vizier, a meeting room with yellow walls, a table and three chairs. We start out the meeting with a simple conversation about the weather on the upcoming weekend. Ed says that he will go fishing for the first time this year; I, in turn, outline my plans for a general clean-up of my apartment over the summer. Conversation with Lewis is incredible—even if I had some concern, now it has gone.

"Maggie, it is good to see you smiling!" Ed glances at his notes, sitting near him on the table. "You had a hard time with Ralph?"

"A little bit! He told me that I was trying to sell the Eiffel Tower to my customer!" I say, excluding the details. No matter how angry I am at Ralph McCarren, I will not put him in the center of an employee intrigue. "The date did not go as I expected. In addition to the Eiffel Tower, I got 'Mr. Customer!'" I laugh, to let Ed know that I perceive this situation as instructive.

"Clearly!" Ed writes down some notes. "Yes, it is pity that you had such a customer. I hope it does not reduce your courage, Maggie. There are many people who cannot pick up the phone and make a call after something like that. You have to realize during the meeting that any other customer could be exactly the same, so the way you prepare is vitally important."

"Others could be just like him?" That starts to worry me. *What if all the customers on the list Ed gave me are the same?*

"Ok, Maggie, how about the progress of your work?"

I present my newly-developed card system, proudly adding that organizing my work like this will improve my productivity.

"I would like you to continue to use the Tamm system." Ed is critical, and it burns my pride in one second. Why did he do that? "Our CRM system is a salesperson's best ally, just like a car is for a driver. Just so you know, in our system I can see what you are doing and how you succeed, and I have noticed that amount of data you enter is minimal. Why is that?"

"The paper version seems easier to me." My shoulders droop, along with the delight on my progress. *Why does everything undermine my confidence that I can do this job?*

"How will you remember what you have to do tomorrow, and what activities you have done with each customer?"

What use is Courageous Maggie to Ed Lewis, if all her achievements are thrown into the playground of Fearful Maggie?

"By the way, we have an unwritten rule,'" continues the boss.

What else?

"If it is not in the system, it has not been done. If I do not see your activities in there the next time, there's no point showing me any paper reports! "

I will not show you anything. You won't understand them anyway!

"So, tell me, what else have you done?"

I have no inspiration and answer the following questions as concisely as possible. I feel deceived and unnecessary. I review statistics about my activities, including how many calls I've made per day and exactly when I make them. Meanwhile, Ed scrupulously records notes about almost every sentence I say. *What kind of cross-examination is this?*

"Is there anything that seems difficult to you?"

I look into his eyes, trying to understand what I should say. I cannot project a bad attitude. I cannot be like a stone. *What should I to reveal to him?*

"As we already discussed, right now my greatest shortfall is making cold calls." I don't want to sound like a wimp and put aside my bad mood. "I would like to start training, finally. The week has passed, but there was no formal training! I would have made greater progress if I had some manuals!"

"Hmm, more *formal* training." Ed continues to write. *He writes your discharge plan*, my insecurity whispers, even though I do not care about it anyway. "Training on specific topics will come later. What would you say if we further define your KPI?" He puts the pen down, and for the first time during this conversation becomes menacing serious.

What is KPI? Pretend to be smart! Is it worth that?

"Yes, I am ready!" I say. *Think Maggie! What? Make up your mind! Why? MAGGIE! Try to be organized! Make up your mind! Run! NO! Fight! Do I exist? Rise up!* Mentally slapping myself, I point out to myself that I already have the salesperson job, and that such details as the boss condemning my note cards will not affect me. *Yes! I will make it on own. I know better!*

"This will allow me to measure your progress in figures as well..." the boss talking in the background. "For me, as a manager, it is important to know whether I can entrust you to work with customers. A three-month test period is actually quite short, so I hope that we can work together."

What is a KPI?

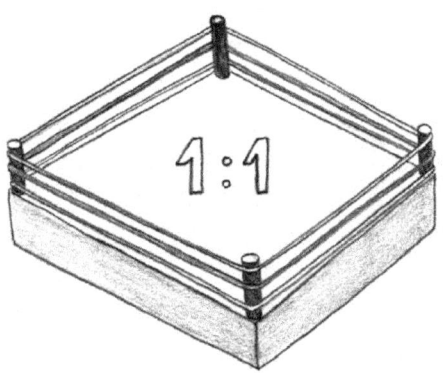

"I expect you to do at least twenty-five meetings per month; that's seventy-five in total during the probationary period." Ed stops to think. "You know, let's make a little less, let's make it sixty dates in total. That should be one of your goals!"

I'm surprised—KPIs are goals! How simple! I write down the figure in my notebook and circle it. *Sixty. Sixty? Dates? That is twenty per month! I will not be able to do it! Is Ed crazy?*

"Second—I am expecting at least five signed contracts by the end of the probation period. For any amount."

Five transactions? With Mr. Customers? How can I possibly do that?

"That is a standard requirement." Ed is direct. "All the salespeople in *Tamm* start with that KPI. It usually filters out those who are willing and able to sell from those who just want to be salespeople."

Thank you, Ed, was that was addressed to me? "Those that just want to be salespeople!" It hurts. I am very afraid that I will not succeed, that the KPI is drastic and inappropriate. *Courageous Maggie, where are you?* I need only one good piece of news, to make me believe that I have not lost my lucky charm on the day when I talked to Ed Lewis in the park.

"You have potential! Just keep on working at it!"

It was a good attempt, and I am trying to recover my motivation. *Standard requirement?* Fear laughs at me. *No, Ed certainly intended those KPI for someone else! He did not mention them in the job interview. How will I manage to get twenty-five dates in one month and five deals in three months?*

"Do not be afraid to use the resources available to you. I am here to help any time if you need me."

I want to hide in the corner and have a rest. The air is stifling in here, and I have a headache. I feel strange. I have been left alone with objectives intended for gods. *Where am I?*

"Our next one-to-one session will be in two weeks, right? I look forward to hearing your results!"

I nod and smile. There's nothing good about this session. Tension finishes me off and I capitulate. White or black. Fear or courage. I want to ask if Ed is a sadist, and involuntarily realize that *I am the problem, not him.* I cannot guarantee results. I do not work the way he needs. In spite of my intentions and my strength being exhausted, I cannot ensure that everything I do will succeed. I am too weak to be the junior salesperson in Tamm Solutions. I am too inexperienced to be able to exceed the KPI set by Ed Lewis.

"I advise you to stay alone for a while." The boss interrupts my thoughts as he stands on the threshold of and observes me.

What?

"Sometimes solitude is the best way to escape from yourself."

I sigh. *What else can go wrong in my short career?*

***

The first week has passed, and I take off my shoes and stretch out on the sofa. Erica is already at home and prepares one of her special meals. She sits down next to me and throws an open magazine in my lap.

"What is it?" I am tired, and reading is the last thing on my entertainment list for tonight.

"Look!" my roommate shows me a circled advertisement. I did not expect that from her, the person who does not like any kind of marketing. "Look, Maggie!"

It turns out that Erica has circled a job advertisement for a translation company that is looking for an assistant project manager. I didn't know that advertisements like this even exist nowadays.

"What do you want?" I ask her, lifting my eyebrows.

"I want you to stop terrorizing yourself!"

"What are you cooking? Can I have some?" I change the topic. Erica is not the right person to ask for advice about a salesperson's professional problems. In fact, right now I do not even want to think about my job.

"Listen, Maggie. I am tired of hearing how you cry into your pillow every night when you came home from the job."

What? By the way, I've cried only twice, I answer in my mind.

"This is your dream job?" *She intends to deeply undermine my thoughts about the future.* "What have you done so far? Made calls like juicer salesperson? Nobody wants to talk to them! But this other job— Maggie, it's convenient for you, and it sounds interesting!"

"Erica, this job is my destiny!"

"Your destiny is crying? I didn't know that!"

"It's just the first week! It's normal that I'm having some problems!" I defend myself, but I do not understand why.

"You will die there," my friend states definitively. She gets up and goes to the kitchen to check that our dinner has not burned.

I will die there. The words repeat in my mind, and I want to pity myself. Instead, I drop the magazine on the table and look at the wall. *Maybe I am naïve, because I believed that I could stand the acerbity and criticism of other people. Maybe I assumed that helping other people is programmed into other people's core values, and now, when I find out that's not true, I have to learn to ask for help— even if it means that I am not as powerful as I had imagined? What exactly is left inside me? The idea that I can adapt the world to my preferences? Love for the profession and striving for excellence? This sales job is not the way I thought it would be, and it has pulled the rug out from underneath my feet.*

What did I expect? "To become a salesperson, you have to forget everything that people think about salespeople," Ed said. Does that mean that I will never get to work with large customers, participate in major conferences and parties on the roofs of New York? *What do I really want? To be a salesperson in Tamm, or to receive gifts such as cars and expensive vacations? Support, admiration, motivation, curiosity?* I cry in the pillow because I do not know who I am, and what I want to do. Perhaps Tamm Solutions is too challenging for me.

I must continue. Yes, what I am able to give to the company during the first week was not as valuable as it could have been, or so it seemed to me. *But I still have the willpower to work on myself and improve. I'm Maggie Kent, and I want to reach top of the sales profession.* Now I need only respect—and the feeling that I am not the customer's doormat. *In fact, not only I have to prove myself that I am a part of the new Tamm generation, but Tamm also has to demonstrate that it deserves to have me work for them—it's a mutual deal.* I know that ridicule, as Ralph looks at me, will not become a part of my nature. I have to understand, if I want to succeed and not become so villainous and arrogant. *Do I want to endure that even in the future?*

"Stop thinking about work." Erica stands in the doorway. "Tamm Solutions ended an hour ago; now forget about it!"

I can't stop myself from smiling. Is everything being so simple for my friend? No worries? No doubts about her self-esteem? No thoughts of what to do with her life? And then I realized that everything could be simple for me too. *I only perceive the current challenges as a punishment that I has been imposed upon me for some kind of violation. But it is not a punishment.* Or is it? I ask myself. *Is it? No, it's not.*

"Dinner's ready," my friend announces.

I clamber off the sofa and stretch my back. I have two beautiful days off to spend in nature with my friends, and I decide not to complain. My destiny... I will wait for a sign that tells me to proceed. But now, my only concern is to have the dinner made by Erica.

The PHARAOH'S CURSE

I'm ready for Monday. The weekend has passed so quickly, and I have not even had time to determine my KPIs or goals or efficiency criteria for my job. I am motivated again! If I have to arrange sixty dates and conclude five deals during the probation period, I shall devote at least 10 hours per week to Ed Lewis in order to reach these goals. If I do not have any training, the boss must replace it with his knowledge! *This is not an ultimatum*, I explain to myself, *it is only what I need to improve my productivity.*

I fill in the information on the Tamm computer system and slip into the chair. Erica will not convince me; being a salesperson position is my destiny, if not in Tamm, then definitely somewhere else. Later I meet Ralph in the kitchen, dressed in a neat suit and with his hair parted on the left. For the first time, I see him looking elegant. Doesn't business etiquette require us to dress professionally?

"Good morning!" I wink. "Meeting with a customer?"

"What?" Ralph is noticeably worried.

"You have dressed up!"

"Me?" he takes a look at his clothes and shrugs. "Maybe!"

"Hey," I take a cup of espresso coffee from the coffee machine, "I thought that we could hold another table tennis session! When you're back, of course."

"I don't think that's possible."

"Why not?"

"We do not work together," Mr. Unbearable retorts. "My responsibilities don't include fawning around you!"

"What?" I hesitate. *I am not asking him to do my work!* "You misunderstand…"

"I understand everything," Ralph interrupts. "Maggie, nothing personal, but working with naive and stupid salespeople does not interest me!"

"I don't understand." I miss a breath. It seems that all the effort I made over the weekend to keep myself in Tamm has been worthless.

"Are you deaf?" Each word he says is solid and full of bitterness. "I do not have time, sorry!" He tries to walk past me, but I grip his sleeve.

"How dare you!"

"How dare *you* say that you have not had training!"

"What do you mean?" I release Ralph's sleeve. *Is he upset?* "I..."

"Don't, Maggie! *You* have not done anything wrong!" he hisses.

"Sorry! But I'm talking about formal training, offered by Tamm! Your support is very important to me!" I defend myself, although my intuition says that will not help.

"Damn it, can't you hear what I say? Stop wasting my time if you can't use it!"

"Ralph, I really do not understand!"

"Maggie, formal training, as you call it, does not exist! There is only team training, led by Ed!" Ralph takes a breath. "Your training —*the real training*— began as soon as you stepped over the threshold of Tamm. Right at that second! No later! The fact that you say you haven't had any training is a slap in the face to all the salespeople who adopt rookies on their team! You stand in front of us, thinking by yourself and your own ambitions, and expecting us to put everything in front of you on a silver tray!"

"I ..."

"When you were talking, I said to play, and you did not do it! You were swimming in your ego and expected to beat the whole team after just one month! Don't say it wasn't like that! You only had *I, I, I. Me, me, me!* Give *me*, help *me*! How will *I* learn! How will *I* make a cold call! How will *I* host the meeting! So much "I" that I'm getting sick! Where is *your* contribution? Not for yourself, but for the team, and understanding the customers, even product improvement? You have some understanding, but you don't have the most important characteristics that a good salesperson must have!"

"You accuse *me*!" I press my fingers into a fist to help me hold back tears. *I will not cry in his presence!*

"This drawing on the wall, where the words 'courage' and 'fear' are written—how often do you look at it? Maybe it is worthwhile to write down the word 'vanity?'"

"What a horrible thing to say!" I feel pressure in my chest and my legs are so tense that it seems as if I'm rooted in the floor, unable to move.

"If you do not understand, drastic methods need to be applied! Do you remember anything that anyone has said to you? Anything? By me or Ed? There are many books on our bookshelves that could help you to become a better salesperson. Have you taken even one and read it?"

Ralph has humiliated me, and there is no one who dares to speak up and save me.

Shut up, Ralph! How can I work here, with someone like this?

"Maggie, can you tell me this? You have learned where everyone sits, but exactly how does that help you to sell more?"

I look at Ralph and clench my teeth. *Monster!*

"How will you be able to speak with customers and coworkers if you ignore all of us? You do not belong here, Maggie. And now, excuse me. I have finalized a deal today!"

Ralph leaves after that parting shot. I run to the toilet in order not to humiliate myself even more in front of the rest of the sales team. Mr. Unbearable has offended me, hurt me so deeply that I do not know whether I will be able to heal. *How could he say something like that? From the very beginning I tried to do my job and follow his advice. How he can call me deaf? How can he call me egotistical, when he is full of arrogance and sarcasm? Are real salespeople being like him? Would they climb over dead bodies? Don't they know pain?* I doubt that in this case we are on route to working together.

I look in the mirror. The workday has just begun, but my eyes are red from crying. *Are you going to let Ralph make you feel like this?* I ask myself. *Fight. Show your character!* My fears are stronger, now they are stronger, in fact. I do not know what to do.

*

Ralph McCarren's outburst is the final straw. I do not want to be here anymore. *I tried. I have learned.* I realize that I'm never going to be useful to Tamm. I should tell them.

After lunch, when I have calmed down and everyone is celebrating Ralph's current deal, I feel ready to talk to Ed. Before leaving the sales office, I look at Mr. Unbearable. He smiles ironically at me, anticipating that I'm going to do. Clearly, he has foreseen that. I even would like to smile at him and say that I regret that he needed to pamper me, but I realize pretty quickly that my amateurish approach would be his greatest pleasure. Ralph has no heart.

I meet Ed Lewis in his office. It is a surprisingly small room with a desk, shelves and still-life paintings of vegetables on one wall. In fact, the cabinet is tasteless; no wonder he chooses to see guests in or Vizier. The boss is already waiting for me with his notes on the table. It is difficult for me; however, there is no other way out. If I stay here, I will start to hate all of them. If I stay here, everybody will start to hate me. Whatever opinion I have of Ed, sales, and my suitability for this position, I will not be able to overcome my intense dislike of Ralph. Erica was right. Mom was, too.

"Please," Ed points to the chair on the other side of his desk. "How can I help?"

I remember this morning, when after the weekend and careful reflection I decided to give myself one more chance to succeed in Tamm. Now, that does not seem to fit into this conversation. I want to get rid of the burden, which I cannot tolerate any more.

"Maggie, I know about your fight with Ralph this morning."

Of course. It couldn't be otherwise, could it?

"Before we agree on any further actions, I want to hear your story. Let's talk."

"He humiliated me, that's the only thing I can tell you! I don't even know why he hates me!"

"No one hates you, Maggie. Ralph will not like you; get used to it. He admits that the only two people who like him are his wife and daughter. That's all! No one else. It's not your fault, that's just how he is! He tolerates me because I am still his boss."

This is not an excuse for Ralph's behavior. I get the feeling that Mr. Unbearable has no moral principles! And, possibly, Ed doesn't either, if he can repeat all I have said to other people, like he did with the "formal" or "non-existent" training.

"Look at me!" Ed leans on his elbows, a little closer to me. "Fortunately for us, Ralph has skills that make him a great salesperson, and he is much better than what you've seen so far. You will also have to learn those skills, in order to become a salesperson."

I lower my eyes.

"What we have here is the story of '*The Pharaohs Curse.*" Ed gets up, goes to the window and thinks. *What is this story about?* I remember that Ralph mentioned something, but at that time I was so angry that I did not ask what it meant. "It tells of a pharaoh who has just ascended to the throne. He is strong, quick-witted and educated, but on the day when the gets the power and gives privileges, he forgets all wisdom of his family, who taught him that only those who listen and are humble gains of the Gods' eternal love. The new pharaoh thought that he knew better, although slowly he plunges into a world that is completely different to the way his people lived. He does not understand. He does not hear, because his ears are closed to what people tell him. He does not see, because his eyes cannot distinguish between the colors. He does not talk, because his mouth doesn't know how to say the right words. The pharaoh becomes a pale reflection of the person he was in the past."

The story is instructive, but what do this have to do with me?

"Salespeople also listen! They soak up information from the potential customer. Maggie, they listen because that is an intoxicating feeling for a customer—to be heard, and to know that somebody cares about them! Ralph succeeds because he is an excellent listener."

Can we stop praising Ralph? I'm not interested in it.

"And what are you doing again?" he asks, sitting down.

"What?"

"You hear, but you don't listen! You don't participate in the conversation and do not ask questions. You do not gain new knowledge. You focus only your thoughts and make counter-arguments in your mind to defend yourself. Maggie, I asked Ralph to confront you this morning."

"What?" I twitch. *My humiliation was staged?*

"I wanted to find out if you would listen in a tense situation, or whether you would stay in your own mind. How do you feel?"

"Bad. Betrayed!"

"Do you want to know how I feel?"

I'm stunned. *You were not ridiculed, Ed.*

"Yes, why would *you* want to know?"

I turn slightly turn red and bow my head. Would I like to know? Oh no! My anger gradually dims, and a feeling of guilt appears. *I hear but do not listen? No, that's not so!*

"Salespeople are also humble," Lewis continues. "Their skills go into the background. They have the skill to disappear, but still be alongside. The salesperson is never the center of attention! You, of course, have ambitions and a desire to achieve something, but don't take that with you to the customer. Everyone feels and uses vanity. Everybody will do it if they see that you come into the office with your head held high, feeling like the ruler of the world. You are making yourself invulnerable, and that arms the customer. Humility, in its turn, disarms. And I'm not talking about weakness, but of humanity and reverence! Maggie, what is the most important thing in *Tamm* for you—you, the company or the customer?" The boss looks at me. "Allow me to ask, how many times at the beginning, middle or at the end of a conversation with me, customers or Ralph, have you showed yourself as a human whose own ego is not the primary issue?"

Sigh. I feel awkward. *I only spoke about the product with Vincent, and I have always considered Ralph to be my competitor. I didn't even say "thank you" when he helped me. Now, what do I think of Ed?*

"People who do not live according to their own assumptions, and who want to learn, listen and see, are called 'pharaohs' in our team. When they do not want to do so, it becomes their curse. A curse that allows no success! Ralph told me that you mentioned this term, but during the week you have not asked what it means.

"Why didn't you tell me what I did wrong?" My heart fills with reproach. *I did not know. I know nothing.*

Listening. Humility. Where has all this disappeared? Was it ever there at all? On the day when I intended to prove myself, I left all that on the doorstep. Shame on me!

"Don't model yourself, Maggie! None of the customers are interested in how beautifully you are able to tell them about Tamm. Allow them to model themselves! Hear and hold on their story!"

I do not belong here.

"How do you feel now, Maggie?"

"Confused. Puzzled. Sad. Impetuous! I wanted to become a salesperson so much that I went the wrong way."

"I have expectations of you."

"Don't!" I straighten my back.

"What?"

"Do not put your expectations on me! I don't know if it is worth it!"

"Maggie!"

"I feel so stupid! I tried to prove myself, and I wanted to do better, but the result was the same! I wanted to argue about KPI, to ask for at least ten hours per week of training with you, in order to achieve the KPI!"

"Then say so!"

"I do not know—or don't want to. Can I be a good employee? Do I have sufficient motivation? I miss the idealism and positive emotions that directed me. Now, there is only sadness and depression. Working at Tamm is too hard for me!"

"What do you want to say?"

"I don't belong here! You need a person who is more responsible. I want to quit!"

My heart breaks. I want to cry. I had only strength for one week, and now I am ready to give up. Ed sits back and rests his hands on the table. He is watching me, just as a doctor watches a patient with an abnormality.

"What did you say?"

"I want to quit," I repeat slowly. "This work is not that I thought it would be."

"What did you think it would be like?"

"I don't know! In general, do not understand the salespeople...what they are, and if I can be one too. If I want to be a salesperson." I pause and look at Ed to see if there is any sign of sympathy of understanding. "Would you believe me if I tell you that my dream is completely different from reality?"

"Yes, I believe it." Lewis holds out a hand across the table.

Farewell already? Even now he isn't trying to keep me here as a salesperson for Tamm. *Is this the future planned for me? The one where I work hard without being giving an opportunity? The one where my attitude is condemned, but at the same time they do nothing to imagine themselves in my position?* I have been accused, and I feel disappointed.

"Fantastic!" he says, as if it was the best news of the day. "Now that you have gotten rid of your dreamy ideas, we can really start the work!"

What is he talking about? I put my hands behind my back, making it clear that I won't shake his hand.

"I have to admit that I have eagerly waited for this moment. Not to get rid of you, Maggie, but in order to understand the weak points that we have to work on." The boss examines his notes. "Salespeople are a strange species, it's true! Now you will not believe that everyone arrives in Tamm with their ideas about the sales profession; and I will not lie if I say that mostly, their ideas are wrong. It is difficult to work with them. For you to do your work, Maggie, I need you be like an empty sheet of paper. I've achieved what is necessary. You have successfully overcome the pharaoh's curse!"

Is Ed Lewis crazy? What is going on? Run! Fear, please get out of my consciousness! Not only the dispute this morning was staged, but everything that happened last week? Really?

"Don't be surprised. No one has betrayed you. Everything you did was as true as the fact that you want to quit." He pauses. Now, do you want to see what you can become?"

I frown. *This doesn't make any sense. I just resigned, and he approved it, right?*

"Are you ready to sell for real, and not just copy old, borrowed clichés?" Ed asks me.

"What are we going to do?"

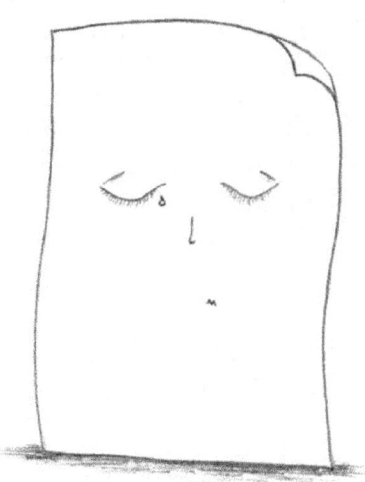

FINALLY YOU ARE
A BLANK SHEET OF PAPER

"We will continue to *build you*. We will give you knowledge, and you will review it and decide if it is good or bad. You will get to work on your excessive emotionality, lack of humility, deafness and shamelessly great love of the comfort zone! You work with on your inability to listen and ask questions. You work with all the resources available to you."

He stops speaking for a moment and looks me in the eye. "Do you want to achieve success in this profession?"

Blankly, I stare back at Lewis. *Are there hidden cameras here, so they can make fun of Tamm's employees?* I do not believe anything he says. *This day has been too complicated for me, and the only thing I want is to make the heartbreak go away. Doesn't he understand that?*

Yes, I want to be a salesperson and achieve success! Everything lights up inside me when I think about it. I would like to try, but I am afraid that it will lead me the wrong way, and that in the end there will not be any benefit. I respect Tamm's achievements, but choose to go further.

"If not, then my perception of you will turn out to be wrong!" the boss says, bitterly. "For a minute, forget what your fear is trying to tell you. Forget your resentment. Incomprehension. Annoyance. Ralph. Me. You. Keep only your tamed ambition, which day after day made you come here and do the work, stand up to your fear and make cold calls, go on a date, lose customers—and still keep going. You want to give up when your imagination turns into reality, and hope that in another place it will be better? It won't be. Not just because Tamm is the best place you could be, but also because where ever you work, exactly the same things will be required of you. And you will have the same weak points that will constantly affect you. Think about it!"

"Ed!"

"I expect to see you here at work, tomorrow." He gets up and gathers his notes. "In addition, this week I will lead training on value mapping for the entire team. It is a theme I have been working on for some time, and it will make the sales process more personal. It will be very helpful! By the way, Maggie, value mapping was one of the reasons why you got this job."

Sigh. *I have to try, to see life from the other side. I am going to follow, or not to follow his advice, with all the ensuing consequences? Should I put my resignation on a distant shelf, so I never see it again? NEVER! No, allow it to remain on the table. Maggie, what are you going to say?*

***

I am on the pier of Coney Island, and the sun is reflected in the clarity of sea and the heat changes with gusts of wind. A long road starts easily, firmly holding me on the pier and giving me an opportunity to enjoy the magic of the sea horizon. The beginning, it seems, is the simplest part of the road, because only then do I feel powerful, rising up in front of the whole world. It says that I have made the right decision. Raising up my sales in my daydream, I let my feet bring me to the finish line, because I have confidence that I will succeed.

True, as I go farther, the pier becomes more unpredictable. Wind and rain and waves have battered the pier making the surface almost impassable. At the moment, I am not looking forward; I am checking the walkway under my feet, carefully. Then I realize that the obligation entrusted to me has turned into a game with time. Courage and skill help me safely through roughness.

I can see my mistakes. I can turn back or continue to go on and fight, despite the fatigue, the pain in my feet, and my ignorance of coming challenges. I choose to keep on going, although I am afraid that the wind will blow me into the sea, or I will not keep my balance and slip on one of the rough or sloping surfaces. I am very scared, but I choose to continue, because I have promised myself that I won't stop halfway and that I will see difficulties as a new subject to study. If I turn back, I will betray myself.

Did the pier intend that? To assess me and my fighting spirit? After taking in the beauty offered by the sea and the sun, I continue on my way, because *this is my choice*. Learning. Adapting. Getting rid of fear and stiffness and becoming free. I get used to the world around me. And I smile. I am glad. I am proud. Not only because I am approaching the finish line of the pier, but also because I am aware that when I reach this finish line, I will not be the same person who stepped on the pier. The pier, of course, will be rougher or smoother depending on where I am at that moment, but I'll go on. I will go on until the end. Without stopping.

I am sure that Tamm Solutions is my pier. I'm staying there. And any fear is powerless in front of my desire.

The Value Map

Jauntily entering the sales office, I meet Ralph at the bookshelf. He tips his head to one side. He has already apologized for the attack in the kitchen, pointing that it was the only way who to get me started on another foot. Three days have passed since this event, and I am not angry anymore.

"Hi! What's new?" I ask, tapping my fist on his arm.

"Today, three new customers have contacted us from the online advertisements! I have to arrange appointments."

"Three! Good luck!" I take the book *Eat That Frog,* written by Brian Tracy, out of my bag and put it on the shelf. "Hey, when will I be able to work with the incoming requests?"

"Maggie, become the senior salesperson, then let's talk about it! Now eat *your* frog and make the calls!"

He noticed the book.

Ralph points to the clock.

I am squinting my eyes. Under the influence of Tracy's book, the frog has become the alert symbol for Tamm's employees. It reminds us that the most difficult work should be done in the morning, so the rest of the day will be free from thoughts of unfulfilled tasks and be much more productive. Also, to get rid of this caprice, the office has bought a small toy frog that is put on the desk of any salesperson who has not done any significant work for more than a week. For me, the frog I have to eat is the phone directory. I go to my desk, which still is near the printer and the water cooler, and notice that there is a certain toy on my table, for the first time. Thank you!

Logging on to my computer, I open my calendar. The date with Dolet Steel three days ago was a failure, and I hope that the value mapping session Ed is teaching at 4 p.m. today will help me to get better results. I am impatient to learn more. *This will be the keystone of how we sell Tamm*, Ed preaches. Searching on Google has not revealed any logical explanation for this term, but it should definitely be something

important! So significant that even Ralph, the person who knows everything about sales, is waiting for this session.

My thoughts are interrupted by a sound, and at first, I do not understand what I am hearing. On returning to reality, I see that Anna is ringing the salespeople's bell. A new deal has been completed! The entire team applauding, and I also express my congratulations. I smile without resenting the fact that it is not my moment of fame and that I am not in my coworker's place.

My turn to hold the mark of achievement for salespeople will also come. It will be my peak, the most celestial expression of my efforts.

***

There has never been so much hustle and bustle in Pharaohs. Ralph is explaining to Carl at what point he would have to say *no* to a customer, but Anna speaks on the phone so loudly that half of what Mr. Unbearable is saying disappears into nowhere. That's ok. I will ask Ralph about it later.

It's four o'clock, and a few seconds later Ed enters the meeting room. I am taking the seat closest to the whiteboard. Although I am trying to calm down, my heart beats fast. I want to know what Ed will say. I feel like a child who has come to a candy factory to taste something unprecedented.

'Thank you for arriving on time," Ed smiles ironically. "I have the pleasure of seeing such a punctual sales team! I appreciate that!"

That makes me laugh. Of all Tamm's salespeople, Ed stands out for having the utmost punctuality, and his remark indicates how disciplined we should be at work.

"Today is a beautiful day. Let's learn the concept of thinking that, I have decided to introduce in our company. Believe me, after today every one of you will sell in a completely different way!"

Silent whispers rustle in the room, and Ed Lewis needs only five seconds to completely enjoy them.

'How do you like Warren Buffet?" he asks rhetorically. "He is the author of the quotation, 'the price is what you pay, but value is what you get.' This quote led me to think about the value of our products. What does the customer obtain when they purchase our CRM?"

Pharaohs is filled with silence. I look at the others, and especially Ralph. I have a suspicion that he might know the answer but has been admonished not to talk.

"Your new selling Bible, my friends, will be the value map!"

We begin. My mind is joyous as I open a new page in my notebook. If this knowledge truly is revolutionary, my sales results should turn around one hundred and eighty degrees. *Focus*! I lock any doubt in the further part of my brain. I write the headline on the top of page and watch Ed.

A moment later a table with four major categories is in front of us, and the boss is watching us cautiously. I am sitting with my eyes wide open and waiting to see what will happen.

TAMM VALUE MAP

FUNCTIONS	SOLUTIONS	CHALLENGES	PEOPLE

"Tell me, what features of our software do you know about?"

"Calendar, reports, invoices," I say, and Ed writes them in the Function column. I know them by heart and could name them even in the dead of night. At least I have gained one benefit from working with Mr. Customer—I am probably the third smartest person behind Ed and Ralph, who can talk about our CRM for hours.

"Tasks, projects, cloud, expenses," Anna takes the baton.

I am looking around at my coworkers' flashing eyes, and I bet that I look the same way. We are created for this product!

"Orders, data importation," I say, feeling like I'm in a competition to determine the champion of the functions. "Mass e-mail!"

"Enough!" Ed raises his hand. "I see that you have very good knowledge of our product's functions."

Great satisfaction and self-esteem wave rustles Pharaohs, surrounding me as well. I like it.

TAMM VALUE MAP

FUNCTIONS	SOLUTIONS	CHALLENGES	PEOPLE
CALENDAR REPORTS INVOICES TASKS PROJECTS CLOUD EXPENSES ORDERS DATA IMPORT MASS E-MAIL			

"The rules are as follows." Ed is authoritative and perfect. No wonder that he is a sales guru. "You should not mention any of these until we have completed the value map," he says, and passes a finger across the Functions bar.

"Oh!" the salespeople snigger. *Why not? Again, I tune in to my coworkers' facial expressions. This milestone has intrigued all of us. But now I sense another irony. From where I am sitting, I cannot freely explore my coworkers' reactions. Why did I choose to sit here? I could dislocate my neck!*

"Why do we refrain from mentioning them?" Lewis stands on the other side of the board. "Because functions have nothing to do with value!"

Don't the functions make the product special?

"Please tell me what kind of people see our product?" Ed points at the last column of the value map, with the title "People."

"The leaders, salespeople, sales managers." This time Carl reveals the list.

'The marketing experts, consultants, IT professionals," adds Anna.

"Who else?" the boss asks. "What would you write, Maggie?"

Me? I turn red, and now I am glad that have taken the seat in front, hence my ignorance can be seen only by Ed Lewis. In my opinion, Carl and Anna have mentioned everyone involved. *Think. No, they have not mentioned everyone!*

"Secretaries also use our calendar," I exclaim. "Secretaries, along with their bosses, are capricious beings, but 99% of the time they pick up the phone and start the conversation with us."

'Thank you, Maggie! Let's not forget that we must not mention the functions."

I frown, feeling as if the teacher had reprimanded me in front of the class. *Focus!*

Ed records secretaries at the bottom of column.

"It looks promising. This is a great list! Have we forgotten any significant person?"

There is silence in Pharaohs. I use my pen to poke at the section labelled "People" on the value map, but I have no ideas. Secretaries, apparently, are the only parties involved who I could imagine.

"Do business owners have a place here?" the sales guru asks, scratching behind one ear.

"Yes!" Ralph bellows. "How could we forget them? They are the biggest beneficiaries of reports!"

Features no, I sigh, watching the reactions to Ralph. *Oh, no!* I take a look at Ed, who sends a critical gaze in the direction of my coworker. *Can Mr. Unbearable also make a mistake?*

"Sorry, no functions!"

I smile. Not because Ralph has been criticized by Ed's a punishment for violating the rules. *Do you see, Maggie,* I'm pointing to myself, *Ralph also makes mistakes? He also learns, just like me. Excellence requires work! Do not be afraid...*

TAMM VALUE MAP

FUNCTIONS	SOLUTIONS	CHALLENGES	PEOPLE
CALENDAR			OWNERS
REPORTS			MANAGERS
INVOICES			SALESPEOPLE
TASKS			SALES MANAGERS
PROJECTS			MARKETING EXPERTS
CLOUD			CONSULTANTS
EXPENSES			IT PROFESSIONALS
ORDERS			SECRETARIES
DATA IMPORT			
MASS E-MAIL			

Ed adds the business owners at the very top of the list. Only now do I notice that he deliberately has left more space there, as if foreseeing that we will forget about the owners. I cannot believe that he knows us so well. It's not possible!

"Great! How do you feel?" Lewis carefully over around the team and nods. "Is everything clear so far?"

I do not understand why we are not talking about the features. Now, when we find out our customer's needs, we can offer Tamm. How can we say that the calendar will allow the supervisors and managers to monitor all the employees' tasks in one place if we are not allowed to mention it?

"Now the most interesting part begins! Let's play!" Ed continues, and his face brightens. "Imagine that you are the owner of a company. What are three key points related to your business that you worry about, that keep you awake at night?"'

"Profit!" I exclaim, raising my hand simultaneously.

'Yes!" says the boss and writes it down on the top of the "Challenges" list, without leaving any free space.

The features of the CRM are left in the background, and I hope that my questions will be answered later. Meanwhile, I cheer and allow myself to swim in the frenzy.

My colleagues are guessing what might be next. Cash flow, credit, risk reduction, growth, business value, cost reduction. I listen and rejoice at the human resources surrounding me. "Eyes, mouth, ears," Ralph has already mentioned. *What will spring from this work*? Now I began to realize its significance. I was so busy sinking in The Pharaoh's Curse that I did not notice that I was able to deal with my problems much earlier. I simply had to learn to open my mouth. We agree that the second key point should be risk reduction and the third, growth.

The role-playing game continues, and we search for the challenges of the other parties involved. That confuses me. I am beginning to realize why challenges are so important, but this total immersion exceeds the things that I've done so far. Now I do not even think about Raymond

Vincent, but about flowers in the market. *Is there is a possibility to sell roses on a completely different level? Does the value is hide there? What do you say, Maggie?*

TAMM VALUE MAP

FUNCTIONS	SOLUTIONS	CHALLENGES	PEOPLE
CALENDAR		PROFIT	OWNERS
REPORTS		RISK REDUCTION	MANAGERS
INVOICES		GROWTH	SALESPEOPLE
TASKS		PRODUCTIVITY	SALES MANAGERS
PROJECTS		CONTROL	MARKETING EXPERTS
CLOUD			CONSULTANTS
EXPENSES			IT PROFESSIONALS
ORDERS			SECRETARIES
DATA IMPORT			
MASS E-MAIL			

'Thank you. That was exhausting!" Ed smiles. "We have filled in almost everything, right? Only the last section remains, and I want you to tell me, based on the challenges we have just written down, what solution we can offer to each of them!?"

"Challenges?" Carl repeats.

"Yes!"

This will be interesting.

"What do you think goes along with the profits?"

"Financial management," says Mr. Unbearable.

"Thank you, Ralph," the boss writes a note in last free column, "Solutions."

"Growth matches with the sales management!" says Anna.

"And time management," Carl adds. "Resource management too!"

"In order to minimize the risks, business protection and knowledge is important," comments Ralph, while Ed writes everything down.

I lean forward to see better. I cannot think of anything that would fit in the "Solutions" column, but the words expressed by my coworkers are alarming. I am like the student who waits for the teacher to fold all the points and explain the connecting element that would make all four columns logical. So far it is difficult for me to understand how exactly to use Ed's value map to sell the CRM, but I am sure that our sales guru has kept something grand for the ending.

"We have successfully reached the most significant moment." The boss comes closer. "This is a value map of Tamm! As you may have guessed, all these columns interact with each other. Can you tell me which columns are the most important on the date with the customer?"

I raise up my hand.

"Maggie?"

'The first and second! Functions and solutions!"

TAMM VALUE MAP

FUNCTIONS	SOLUTIONS	CHALLENGES	PEOPLE
CALENDAR	FINANCIAL MANAGEMENT	PROFIT	OWNERS
REPORTS	SALES MANAGEMENT	RISK REDUCTION	MANAGERS
INVOICES	TIME MANAGEMENT	GROWTH	SALESPEOPLE
TASKS	RESOURCE MANAGEMENT	PRODUCTIVITY	SALES MANAGERS
PROJECTS	BUSINESS PROTECTION	CONTROL	MARKETING EXPERTS
CLOUD	KNOWLEDGE		CONSULTANTS
EXPENSES			IT PROFESSIONALS
ORDERS			SECRETARIES
DATA IMPORT			
MASS E-MAIL			

"Maggie, unfortunately, the greater part of salespeople lives for that. Why? Because it is convenient! It is a comfort zone for salespeople. The problem is that customers do not understand that!"

I sink back in the chair, looking at Ed's value map with a small dose of disbelief.

"That's ok, Maggie, don't worry! It is natural to think that we sell functions! Therefore, we are here to become better! In fact," he comes to the board and makes a spiral line, connecting the Solutions and Challenges columns, "the real sale is going on here! Here is the value!"

Pharaohs relapses into silence again. This time it is an excited silence. The faces of my coworkers show both surprise and admiration at the same time. Everyone is waiting for what Ed will tell us. Me too!

"When a customer does not see the value, it does not matter what features can we offer!"

"Why?" I ask.

"Imagine that you are manager of a small creative agency. I call you and say that we have a CRM system that can improve the agency's business processes. What your reaction be? Why should I listen to you? Of course, you would ask how you can improve it. And I, being proud that I know all details of the product, shall say that the we will provide an invoice dispatch function and a calendar for monitoring the employees' work flow. Maybe I will list some more functions to sound more impressive, although I have no idea what you need, or whether you need any of them. How appropriate would that will seem to you, Maggie?"

"Not very!"

'How can they be interested in our software if they have not even seen it?" Ed drastically cuts away my usual sales habits. "How can they be interested if you do not speak their language? Never try to sell our software on the phone; they will not buy the Eiffel Tower. Focus on challenges and solutions!"

"How?"

"Let's use the same conversation as an example. I call and say that I want to arrange a meeting about how we can improve the agency's productivity. How would you react this time? You'd be curious fur sure, and you would ask how we can improve our productivity. I would say that I represent a company that cares about your business efficiency, and during the meeting you will be able to learn how time management and sales management can help you to identify business risks, increase your employees' productivity, and in particular, to accelerate your business growth. How appropriate will I seem to you now, Maggie?"

I discover that I am sitting with my mouth open.

"Very appropriate!"

"Is value what the customer actually obtains by purchasing our CRM?" Ed asked that at the very beginning. I stare at the value map so closely that I could burn a hole in it and try to understand. *Is this the way to a customer's heart?* Grandma suddenly appears in front of me, with her flowers and the people who came back to her again and again. For Grandma's customers, the flowers were also Grandma's warmth, trust, kindness and honesty. Flowers were the interlocutor they recognized in Grandma. Value! It was something more, that formed my grandmother's business card and made her to be popular in the whole marketplace. "The value map is one of the reasons why you got this job," the boss had said, and now I remember that I told him about it in the job interview. From an early age I knew about the value, but for some reason hadn't really understood it! I laugh inside myself. *Thank you.*

"Always remember that Tamm is in your hands, and that can completely change the development of the customer's business!" Ed points to the board. "Help them to understand. Listen! Explain. Show them the value! Use words that they care about and earn their confidence. And when they are ready, conclude the deal!"

I want to plunge into the sea of values and pull out the treasure that will be used in every phone conversation and on every date. Not the calendar, but time management. Not the projects, but sales management. Not data input, but business intelligence. I want to sell the way Ed taught us. Finally, I have received the winning recipe!

The Boiler House

"No, we are not interested in that." The secretary answers me in a shrill voice, and I put down the receiver. Why? I am fed up with it! Really! After the value map training my calls must be perfect, but I still cannot get out of the swamp of cold calls. When I will earn my star of happiness? *Wait Maggie*, I shush myself, *you will survive*!

I call, and they tell me "no." Again. I call, but nobody answers. This is followed by no, no, no...and again no. After the last refusal, I throw the phone down on the table in anger. *The receiver is not an enemy.* I see the framed card, and I want to hit the person who invented this text. *Stupid calls!* I realize that this part of the job excites me the least. I do not know how sound unbreakable in telephone conversations with strangers. How can I make the secretary understand the value? How do I get to the managers? An alternative weapon, e-mail, suits me best. At least rejection does not hurt so much in an email.

I also get *no* also from the last number on the phone directory page and feel like I have climbed over the obstacle wall. It's true that I have not won this battle, and that makes me sad. And angry. I decide to talk to Ralph; I finally have to deal with this problem.

"What happened?" He mumbles as I stand in front of him. He organizes his desk drawer and does not delve into my feelings. "Has something bad has happened, apart from your sleepy eyes and clothing?"

"What?" I'm startled. "What don't you like about my clothes?"

"You do not look like a professional! If a customer came in now, they would not take us seriously."

Placing my hands on my hips, I lift my chin up. I didn't sleep well, so I chose comfortable, casual clothing. *I didn't think that a shirt and jeans would be seen as inappropriate. Also, today I don't have a date.*

"When I dress up, you tell me it is wrong. When I don't, it is still wrong. I don't understand you."

"You wore your business suit the first day in order to advertise yourself, like a poster! That is a bad motive. I want you to wear it because you never know when you'll have a date with a customer. Clothing is a part of our work, not for the glorification of your ego!"

How can he know my motives for wearing particular clothing?

"Okay, enough about clothes," he hisses; apparently, I am not giving him the reaction he wanted. "How many '*Nos*' have you received?"

Is this the only subject we can talk about?

"A lot! It's always 'No!" Ten of them!"

"Don't worry about it. *No* is the standard answer. Work on 'No' until you get a '*yes!*'"

"I don't understand."

"What is the problem, Maggie?" Ralph inspects the next drawer in his desk.

What is he looking for? Why does he talk to me so indifferently?

"You will often work with a 'no' and then go on to build a relationship. Selling is like that!"

"How can they make a decision so quickly—without even looking at what we can offer?"

'There are a lot of reasons. Calm down and continue."

"Ralph!" I sulk. *I hate Mr. Unbearable's attitude. And I hate that I cannot get a "yes."* "Will you help me to understand what is not working?"

"What is the problem?" Ralph takes a folder out of the drawer, puts it on his desktop, and sneezes. I cannot believe that it is so hard for him to help me. He wins the "best salesperson" title for three months in a row; would one friendly comment be so terrible? "Maggie, stop!"

"I'm pretty far from achieving my KPI, and it annoys me! Even after learning about the value map, I feel like an idiot! I hear "No" all the time! How can I fix it?"

"Will you stop looking at failure as something subversive?" Mr. Unbearable returns to inspecting his drawer. "First of all, stop taking all this so personally! There are things that you can and cannot control. Imagine that you want to buy a dress. You try on all of them, but there's nothing you really want to wear. The salesperson will tell you how great it looks on you, but you tell her that you will not buy it. Why?"

"She cannot control what I like?"

"And the salesperson cannot control what you think," Ralph adds. "You won't agree with the shop assistant just because she wants you to. You have a backbone! You know what you need! Why do you want to control the people you are calling on the phone? Why don't you let them think their own thoughts? You are able to influence, but not control, Maggie!"

"I can only control my own mind?"

"Fortunately, or unfortunately, yes! Only your own thoughts, behavior, plans, dreams, ideas, words—you do not have power over others! So why worry if we cannot change someone else? Worry about things that are really important!"

"And what is important?"

"Second, you have to concentrate. We all have emotions, weaknesses and bad days. Leave your bad mood at home. What will you do if a customer confronts you with such negativity? Will you shout at them? Go to the washroom and calm down! And if you're not going to do that, go away!"

"Then why you are a salesperson, cutthroat? Are your emotions perfectly controlled?"

"Tamm Solutions is not paradise, Maggie. When you are surrounded by a lot of sharks, you cannot afford to be weak! If you do not work on yourself, your emotions will be your headstone in this work!"

"Ralph!" My mind explodes. I cannot stand it.

"What? 'You either win or learn,' —that's what Nelson Mandela said. You should already understand that a salesperson doesn't work in a rose garden. The victories will be only 10% of your job! Yes, you have not been able to enjoy a deal being concluded, hearing the ringing of sales bell here in the office, and praise for your good work. Not yet. And you will spend the remaining 90% of your time to achieve the sales, the victories! You will have to earn them with hard work and repeat it day after day.

"Understand that you lose only when you are able to learn from your own mistakes. Failure is a kind of benefit, because it allows you to draw conclusions. Every refusal can make you better! But you like making experiments, is that it?" He pulls out a black folder and smiles. *So, he was looking for that file.* After a quick glance through it, he drops it on the table.

I blink my eyes. *Mr. Unbearable won't help me?*

"On Monday we will have an intense call session, during which we will clarify your script. Let's finish off these cold calls!" he suddenly says.

"What should I do?"

"Stop making cold calls. Instead, prepare some good contacts that you can use on Monday. Can you do that?"

I sulk, but nod.

***

"We're not a call center. That's one of the reasons why we don't have a call script," Ed says when the sales team has gathered in Pharaohs. "We believe that every salesperson is smart enough to create his or her own scenarios that work—that's another reason why you don't have a call script. Be creative! Tamm does not restrict you!"

This, of course, sounds nice, but does not help my weak skills when I try to arrange dates by phone with potential customers. I lower my eyes and peruse the established list of contacts, in which I have included all 26 numbers of from the phone directory who haven't answered my calls and added another 50 numbers from the textile industry. I am ready, even without realizing it.

"Now you are in the boiler room, or intensive call session!" announces Lewis, and the sales staff of Tamm Solutions becomes more attentive. "What does that mean? Making telephone calls, all day long!"

How can I do that? Anxiety takes over my heart, and I doubt that I will have enough strength to call for so long. I look at my coworkers. The statement does not seem to cause any apprehension in them.

I must not look afraid.

"Today, in the boiler room, we will have three sessions, and each will be two hours long. During this time, you make calls, and that's all! No dreaming. No filing! Nothing else! Only brutal cold calls and making appointment for dates. When the first session ends, you take a break and then continue again. We will record the results here, on the whiteboard."

This is horrible!

"You are four salespeople. How many dates can you set up?"

"Each?" Carl is intrigued and receives an affirmative answer. "I think three dates would be very good!"

"Twelve meetings in total?" Ed shakes his head incredulously. "I would say five for each of you!"

I've never arranged five meetings on one day. The boss writes the numbers from 1 to 20 on the whiteboard, leaving a space beside each number to write the name of company.

"It's time to set higher goals for yourselves. All of you had to prepare at least fifty contacts for today, so five dates out of them is just a trifle!" Ed smiles. "Believe in yourselves! It gives good results! And remember," he points to the board, "your successes will not be forgotten!"

I squint my eyes. *I will not be forgotten for what reason?*

Ed takes a small box from the table and shows it to his salespeople.

'This is a competition. The best salesperson will receive a prize! Do you want to know what is inside?"

"No!" Anna exclaims. "Let it be a surprise!"

"Ok!" Lewis shrugs. "Believe me, the prize is worth it!"

Pushing my fear away. I turn on all my ambitions. I want to prove myself!

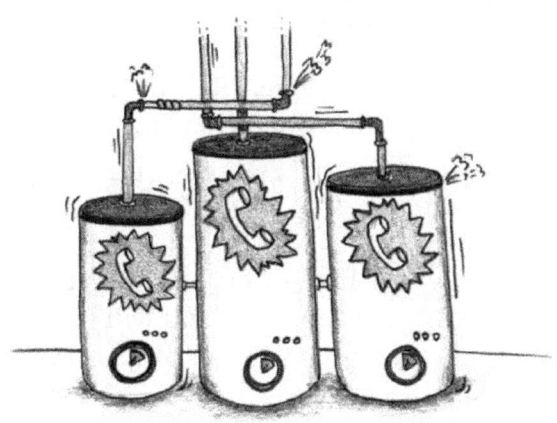

"Maggie," Ed addresses me, "you will work with Ralph. He will teach you a few tricks that will help you to improve your technique. Is that ok with you?"

'Yes," I answer. *At least I am not working on this all alone.*

"It's already ten minutes after ten o'clock. Let's begin!" The boss claps his hands, and Tamm's sales team starts to work.

I spend a moment watching how the others get ready for cold calls. They all become serious and find a more comfortable place. Carl chooses a spot near the windowsill, while Anna takes a chair and places it at the other window. They open their laptops, bring up their lists of prospects and start making calls. With every second *Pharaoh*s becomes louder, the voices of salespeople bouncing off the walls of *Tamm*. I sigh.

"Maggie," Ralph sits down opposite me and opens his laptop, "are you ready?"

I nod, although this movement is rather unconscious.

"Remember the ping-pong method? We'll use it now! You will call, and then I will call! We'll get to your ideal conversation scenario!"

Is it even possible? Pulling my notebook closer, I dial the first number of my twenty-six metalworking contacts. Hearing a beep in the receiver, I switch on the speaker, so Ralph can hear the entire conversation. I sweat. I'm hot. *Value map. What do I have to say?*

"Hello, Distribution Wires!"

"Hello, I'm Maggie from Tamm Solutions! Can I speak with your manager?"

"What do you want to speak about?"

My throat dries out. I am afraid of failure. Again.

"I represent a company that develops CRM systems that would help to improve the growth of your company."

"No, thank you, we don't need it!" the secretary's voice becomes angry.

Not again! This can't be! May I ask why you are not interested in the growth of your company?"

"I cannot give you that information. Thank you!" The secretary terminates the conversation quickly and emphatically. She even does not expect me to answer her.

I hiss and push the phone away.

"We have a first date!" Ed exclaims loudly, applauding Anna and encouraging competition in the boiler room. "Don't wait," he urges the others who pick up their pace and make calls.

"What are you doing?" Mr. Unbearable leans across the table and punches my arm. "Don't worry about the call! It is not your fault that the growth of company is not important to them! They don't care, and their attitude is terrible! That kind of company is not our customer."

I smile, although we both realize that it will not improve my mood.

"Be more confident in yourself. Smile when you talk. Pause. Cold calls are very simple. You started very well—we always need to talk to the manager, or whoever is responsible for the company's development. You don't have to convince the secretary about the fact that they need Tamm."

"But how can I deal with secretaries?" I squeak.

"Exactly as you just did! Ask them to connect you. Stay with your script."

"It is easier to say that than to do it!"

"It will be fine!" Ralph laughs. "Also, don't say 'CRM system'—this term may be too complicated for the customer. Besides, remember that you are selling the opportunity to come on a date inscoffeed of selling Tamm!"

"Why is that?"

"You need an appointment to show the software. Nothing else!" my coworker specifies. "The rest is not important! Give me your next phone number."

I'm tell him the next number on the list, glad that Ralph is helping me.

"Hello, *Polert*!" the secretary answers. I listen carefully to hear what will happen.

"Hello!" Ralph becomes silent, and two seconds pass until he gets a response.

"Good afternoon!"

"I'm Ralph from Tamm Solutions. Could I speak to ..." he looks in the notebook where I have written down the names of the decision-makers, "Sylvia Stanton?"

Sylvia Stanton is the head of Polert's Development division.

"What is the purpose of your call?"

"It is related to Polert's business development and efficiency."

"Wait, please!"

Oh, that was too easy! Mr. Unbearable stands up and walks along the table, exuding manliness, restraint and confidence. There is a beep, and Ralph is connected. *Too easy.*

"Hello!"

"Hello, is this Sylvia?"

"Yes, good afternoon!"

"I am Ralph from Tamm Solutions! I would like to arrange a meeting with you about business development. This will take half an hour, during which you will get insights into how to promote growth and efficiency in Polert."

I smile ironically. *Surely it can't be this easy!*

"How are you going to promote it?" Sylvia's voice is full of disbelief.

"Our company cares about business development, and we want to help you. Tell me, please, have you ever had a situation when your financial resources were not used properly, thus hindering your growth?" Ralph is not intimidated.

"In my opinion, it is part of our daily business!" Sylvia says, perhaps more sharply than she would like.

"And do you ever had a situation where investment is not provided in a timely fashion, and this has slowed down product development" Mr. Unbearable is aggressive. I see how he works with the value map in reality, but I don't know if I can simulate that. Ralph pushes forward like a bulldozer, and it does not matter. Strangely, at the same time, I do not hear any vanity in his voice.

Sylvia is silent, maybe because she has been in this situation. Maybe not. My pulse becomes faster, and I find myself feverishly waiting to hear the result of this conversation.

"At present, you have an opportunity to see how effective resource management and financial planning helps to prepare for such situations and even to completely prevent these situations from occurring. How does that sound to you?"

"That sounds very good!"

"Can we make an appointment next week, on Wednesday, for example, at ten or two o'clock?"

"Wait, I have to look at my calendar."

It cannot be. I frown to myself. *It CANNOT BE!* I take a look at my other coworkers, to check whether they see the same thing as I do and become a little sad when I realize that they are only interested in their own contacts and their own calls.

"Yes, Wednesday at ten o'clock in the morning would be fine!" Sylvia agrees.

"Excellent, Sylvia! I will look forward to talking with you. So, we have agreed to meet next Wednesday at ten o'clock in your office at 48 Bleecker Street, if I understood correctly?"

"Yes!"

"Thank you, have a nice day! See you!"

"Goodbye!"

Ralph hangs up, and I cannot comprehend the simplicity I heard in each second of the conversation. Mr. Unbearable only has to call, and a date is guaranteed. *How does he do it?* My mind stubbornly tries to convince me that it was a coincidence, because the secretaries I have encountered are not as easy to deal with. *How can I do this too?*

"How can I do this too?" I ask aloud, inspired by my coworker's date. Can I also can make a date? Ralph goes to the board and writes the name Polert beside number four and writes my name in parentheses. It is incredible that the Boiler room is filling the list of customer dates so fast!

"Ralph!"

"Number *one*—introduce yourself. Then pause and wait for a response. The secretary will be obliged to talk to you, because you've already listened to them.

"Number two—tell them what you want. And what you want is an appointment. Nothing more! You don't try to sell the product, as I said. If you find yourself heading the wrong way, remember that you need a date.

"Three—tell the customer why he should meet you. Name one or two benefits that he will get from the meeting and go on.

"Four—leave some space for questions and answers. There always be somebody who won't understand, and you can devote your time to answering their questions.

"Again, we do not discuss functions, or the product. If you discover that you are going the wrong way, remember that you need a date. Also, at this point the customer also must understand that they need a date, with high added value.

"Five—agreed on the time of the appointment. Offer the customer two times and let them choose. The ball constantly remains on your side.

"Six—once more, name the exact place and time and let the customer confirm that everything is correct. It shows that you really care about this date. And then, say goodbye."

I quickly record the main points. Now the call scenario looks promising. It's completely different from my attempts to reach a positive outcome. *Was this how Ralph made the call in our first ping-pong session?* I cannot remember.

"Call." Ralph points to the phone. "The boiler room will not wait! Let's get to work!"

The receiver is not an enemy. I take a look at the card that has been placed on the windowsill in the boiler room today, and call.

"Hello," the secretary responds, and I break into the conversation. I follow the advice of my coworker and concentrate on setting up a meeting. By using Ralph's script, I almost succeed. I cannot get through to the date though, and I resign myself to failure. Ralph tells me to call again. Immediately! So, I do, feeling sure that I will get stuck between the secretary and the manager again. "No." I have to call. "No." It looks like Ralph's advice does not work.

"I know what the problem is!" Mr. Unbearable sinks back in his chair. "And it is not the conversation script, or the secretaries, or anything else. It is you!"

I cross my fingers.

"How can you set up a meeting if you do not believe in it? You have so many negative assumptions that they literally can read them in your voice! Maggie, you can tell yourself that you can do it? Otherwise, we won't get out of here for a long time! The people whom you will call, need us. We can make them better. Look at it from the other side. You cannot lose what you don't have!"

"I don't understand that."

"When you call these companies, they are not your customers. You cannot damage anything. There is no relationship. Nothing. The worst thing that can happen at the end of each call is that they still will not be your customers. You'd be at the same place, at the starting point! That's not very nice, of course, but this is the *worst* that can happen! Does that scare you?"

"No!"

"Then why are we still talking? Pick up the receiver and call! Be confident! You will succeed!"

Responding to Ralph's command, I call. I expect to have a victory. Will it be happening?

"*Hello?*" I hear the secretary answer, and smile.

"Hello." I start the conversation and then fall silent, listening for what will come next. My colleague is nodding and continuously encourages me. It gives me the support I need. How easy is it to make a call when you are encouraged by a successful salesperson!

"Good afternoon!"

"I'm Maggie from Tamm Solutions. Can I talk to Olivia Drummond?" give a wider smile. By copying Ralph's conversation, with only a few necessary changes, I get to the manager. I take a breath and continue. My colleague is still nodding, and that keeps me afloat. I am worried, but I try to keep calm. "Good afternoon, Olivia?"

"Yes!"

"I'm Maggie from *Tamm Solutions*. I would like to make an appointment with you regarding business development. This will take only half an hour, during which you will learn how to promote KAM Metals' growth and productivity."

Previously I did not have humility; I've found that now. And after a short conversation, Olivia tells me yes. I hang up, regaining my self-confidence and inner strength. I record this as the sixth date on the board, and it fuels my excitement. I let Ralph make his calls, while I shape my conversation scenario with each subsequent call. At the end of the first session I feel drained, but pleased. The whole team has already made twelve dates. After the second session we reach our daily target—twenty. Tamm's sales force is hungry for further battle, and we close with the third session—with thirty-five dates arranged.

"Who is the winner?" Ed looks at the board when the intensive call session is over and claps his hands together. I also cannot believe the result. "Carl!"

Carl grins. He has arranged eleven dates, outpacing Ralph by two dates. Carl opens the box, and a nice Faber-Castell pen is inside.

"Wow!" Carl is excited. "We should do this more often!"

We all applaud him, and for a minute he is the center of the Tamm world. Meanwhile, I am extremely proud of my five dates. They have changed my cold calling experience beyond recognition. Now, everything is simple. It can be done. *I was afraid, but I am no longer afraid.*

Listening

The park, where my job interview took place, has not changed at all. There are trees, benches, and even some people that I have seen before. Meanwhile, I have become different and, I feel happy and elated. The boiler room has inspired me, and I am ready for new challenges.

"How are you, Maggie?" Ed is sitting on the same bench, just as it was for the interview.

"Great! Hopefully this week there will be news to share," I smile. Metals LLC and Andrew Freeman is on my schedule. I tried to catch them on my first day of cold calling, but it seems that this week it will end with a date. "And how are you, Ed?"

He smiles. I am a good student and have learned to ask questions whenever I notice the opportunity.

"Very good, thank you! I am glad to see you so happy."

I nod with appreciation.

"The reason why we are here is that I wanted to talk to you outside the office. This place seemed to be the most appropriate."

I don't like how that sounds. *Maggie, calm down! I'm not normal, I'm special. Think like that!*

"The well-being of our company employees means a lot to me, and I want to understand what is really happening to you in Tamm. Can I ask a question about that?"

"Yes," I squint, with the sun in my eyes.

'Tell me, has there been any situation during these past few weeks when you felt motivated and self-confident?"

Why is he asking me that? Have I done something wrong?

"Maggie don't be so negative! Free your mind!" Ed leans closer to me. He really is interested in what I will say. I calm down and try to remember the most inspiring moments. *Oh, I know!*

"You will find this wrong and inadequate after all the sales training, but I was very self-confident when I went on a date with Peter Sherman. There I met Raymond Vincent instead— "Mr. Customer." Yes, I was focused on telling a story about *Tamm* and did not ask him any questions, but at the beginning of the day, it seemed to me that everything was finally is going to be ok." I stop and think. That day turned out to be insane and degrading, but now, looking at it through the lens of my training, it was a very valuable experience.

Nobody can take that away from me. "That morning I was focused and promised myself to be a professional, no matter what happened. I listened some motivating *TED* speeches, repeated the *Tamm* functions to myself—how silly of me, right? —and I was ready to conquer the world! I was an idealist, and I believed that it had to be my day!"

The words flow from my mouth, and my boss just listens. That helps me to remember even more.

"Of course, I also relied on Ralph," I began to gesture with my hands, to project the story more expressively. "Although I didn't really like him, I considered him to be my support. It's strange, it feels as if it happened a long time ago. If I were to face the same situation now, I would definitely act differently!" I sighed "Yes, it would definitely be different!"

"What would be different?"

"I would put Negotiations between the columns Challenges and Solutions," I tell him, speaking in terms of the value map. "I would not try to sell the Eiffel Tower and put the emphasis on functions! I did not do the most important thing—I did not discover the customer's problems. I was not listening."

"Let's take a walk," Ed suggests, and I agree. "About listening—let's talk about it in detail! What do you think, does it tend to be stingy?"

"Stingy listening? I've never heard that expression."

We turn onto a small street off the park that runs toward the river.

"The customer's answers, Maggie, will never be stingy. Remember that words said by people, or customers, will never exceed their field of knowledge. For example, if you ask the question, "what was the result of yesterday's basketball game?" to a person who does not follow that game, you can expect a short answer, and probably a very unspecific response. If you ask the same question to a basketball fan, you'll get detailed report on the events of the game. In which case can you can say that the answer is stingy? The first, because he knows nothing about the topic? Or, it may be the second, because he tells you so much that it gives you nothing valuable in the end? You, as a salesperson, are prohibited from putting customers in a position where they feel guilty about the situation, whether they know a little or a lot!

"Furthermore, if you bring certain stereotypes and expectations to the discussion, do not be angry about the answer afterwards. Be angry at your duplicity—that you have listened stingily and have not created enough confidence to make the customer to open up. You will always have only the information that the customer has given to you. Nothing more!"

Stingy listening? Interesting! Do I do that?

"How did you feel when you were talking about your joyful memory in Tamm?" Ed's voice is calm and warm as we continue walking at a relaxed pace.

"I felt proud! The more I told you, the happier I felt, as if I was living through it one more time. Only ..." I look at Ed and blink my eyes. "Only this time, with you, I gave you something nice. I trusted you!"

"Would you have told me so much if I didn't listen to you?"

"I guess not."

"If we do not listen, can we can find out our customer's whole story?"

"I guess not!"

"Perhaps we listen not just to the words, but also to the emotions, where the true customer lies.

"Why?"

"Because after the introduction, there is always a discussion. A great story! That's what we need—the truth!"

"Great, Maggie!"

We turn to go back to the park, and Ed stops. "Keep it up! Now, I want you to go to the couple over there," he changes the subject and points to the young people sitting on the grass. I remember them both; they were also here in the park during my job interview.

He wants me to sell them our Tamm software? Nope!

"Maggie don't make such a face! This is an extremely easy task, believe me. It will only take five minutes! You don't have to tell them anything, just find out everything that this couple thinks about the new farmer's market on Saturdays."

What? The farmer's market is definitely a topic that I know very well. I love to go there myself. No, I don't want to talk to them about it. Perhaps I am looking for a lifejacket in Tamm. I wrinkle my nose, praying that Ed will change his mind, but his facial expression remains unchanged. My fear can be lessened in front of him, but I still need to go to the couple. I take a breath. *Ok, good. Nothing crazy.* I make up my mind and walk towards the unknown.

"Bye," I say, waving to the boss. "Wait for me here!"

***

I sit down on the grass some fifteen feet away from the couple. *Damn it, I will dirty my skirt!* Both of them are enjoying the sun and some strawberries, and my interruption would be nasty violation of their privacy. *Farmer's market*, I think to myself, getting angry that I have such a task.

"Yes?" the guy asks, and I flip. *What?*

"What?" I get confused and put my hand by my mouth. "Oh, excuse me! Am I too close?"

"No," the girl smiles. She has beautiful curly hair that falls across her shoulders.

"No?" I slightly slide away. "Other people usually sit so close to you?"

Terrible! I sound like a maniac. They will immediately call the police and ask them to take me to a padded room!

"What?"

"I asked," seeking a way out of the situation, "because I usually have a box of fruits and vegetables next to me when I come here on Saturdays. I don't mean to interfere. Today, of course, I do not have the box with me, but the habit is still there!"

"Fruits and vegetables?" The girl is confused.

The conversation is complicated and clumsy, but I have come to the topic. *What do I need to learn?*

"Yes, fruits and vegetables. I like them a lot! What do you think of the farmer's market on Saturdays?"

The guy frowns. I can see an enormous distrust in him. I'm not surprised! *How can I get past this barrier? Maybe I need to be friendlier*? I realize that will seem too artificial.

"It's good," the girl says. She apparently feels safe near her boyfriend; that's why she responds so easily. I would feel the same in her place. *The farmer's market? How do I get to that?*

"Maggie!" Ed calls me.

Why? I'm not finished!

"Come on over here!"

I shrug. He's eccentric.

"Excuse me! I have to go," I grin. "Have a nice day!"

"You too!" they both say at the same time.

I quickly get up, check to see if my skirts are dirty, and run to Ed.

"Five minutes have elapsed. Did you talk about the farmer's market?" My boss is curious.

"Yes, and they certainly think I'm a psychopath," I tell him with a wink. "Thank you for that, Ed!"

"Can you tell me what you just did?"

"I tried to find out what they think about the farmer's market on Saturdays! It was not successful."

"What did they say?"

"Mmm... they said..." I cross my arms in front of me and think back to what I just experienced. I have the revelation that I was so busy with the task, and how I must have appeared to them, that I cannot remember very much of our conversation. "Good. The girl thinks that the farmer's market is good," I sigh.

"When you were there," Ed points to the couple, "you were a robot. You performed the task. I would say that you executed it very well, you tried desperately to get to the given theme! You went right by the book. However, along the way you forgot that you also have to listen!"

Yes, I know. Hanging down my head, I agree with his criticism.

"Come on, let's talk!" the boss goes ahead. "Salespeople are not listening. It is the greatest problem of our profession. You have it too. We will get over it!"

***

"Stingy listening is essentially non-listening. Or an imitation of listening," says Ed, by holding his cup of coffee. We've moved from the park to a nearby coffeeshop, and second phase of my training begins. "Learning to hear is easy! Learning to listen is not. You know why? We are accustomed to think in parallel. It's some kind of mental multi-tasking. We think that if we do it that way, we'll do it faster and better, but it's not true. In our work, we can lose any potential customer because we simply will not hear something important!"

"Ed, does that mean that we never hear anything?"

"No! When you spoke about your experience in Tamm, which, incidentally, was the first listening exercise today, I heard only you. I didn't think about what I was going to say, or what comments to make. You were my focus, and every time I found myself going in the wrong direction, I turned around and got myself back on track. The bigger ego we have, more patient need to become and the more difficult it is to return.

"How important was that I listened to you?"

"Very!"

"Imagine what it means to the customer!"

Ed is right.

"A salesperson is allowed to speak, but do not interrupt. You can go from the general world to the deepest one. It has explicit, high added value, which will be the biggest trump card, once you have earned it! Is this the sense of a good conversation? A good salesperson does not speak, but only listens! Listening has one more nuance that makes thinking of sale human and humble!"

"What is it?"

"I want to tell me the saddest event in your career in Tamm."

"The saddest?" My face changes. *No, I do not want to talk about that.* That includes emotions, and I know how skeptically Ed and Ralph refer to the state of my soul at critical times.

'This story will remain just between us." The boss drinks his coffee. "Don't you trust me?"

"Yes!" I sigh. "I remember that day. It was on Monday, when Ralph told me that he would never work with me. He said a lot of destructive things, and I took refuge in the toilet, crying." My chin trembles, a tear runs over my cheek. I have not talked about it, even with Erica, hoping to erase it from my memory or at least mitigate the hopelessness of that day. However, it is right here, disguised as a dull spear that can still destroy me. That day, Maggie was dead for a few minutes. "For me, it was too harsh, especially coming from Ralph. But I don't know if I would act differently if he repeated it. I usually cry when somebody hurts me, because it is the only way to get rid of pain. I felt powerless, and without any plans for the future. I felt alone." I wipe my cheek and smile, helping the boss to think that I am not angry at him for this gamble.

"Thank you, Maggie! Thank you for sharing that. I appreciate it. How do you feel now, when I listened to you talk about that event?"

"Naked! I did not have any shield and I put the weapon in your hands, and you could have hurt me! It was not like telling you about the happy time, the nice moment when I willingly shared my memories with you. This time, there was a secret, and it hurts...and, probably, I feel ashamed. This was something extremely intimate! This memory could destroy me if you decide to use it against me."

"So, what is important to you?"

"That I can trust you! Without this connection, I would never reveal something like that!"

"Can you link it to sales?"

I sit in the coffee shop, thinking.

"Customers come to us at their saddest moments, don't they? They are proud of the success and professionalism of their company. It is the beauty and glory that they have worked for, twenty-four hours a day, seven days a week, and it has unsolved problem! The problem is, they are likely to blame themselves for decisions they have made or rejected. It is our duty to listen to them, and help!"

I take a breath. *I made this mistake in the conversation with Vincent. I was so worried about myself that I did not pay attention to his story. I did not build the basis for trust.*

"What will you do when you have your next meeting?" Ed asks, drinking his coffee. I haven't touched my cup yet.

"I will go without any stereotypes. Without any assumptions that I know what they need. Finally, I will let them talk!"

"Great, Maggie!" My boss winks at me. "Let's finish this discussion with the last task. A woman in a red dress is sitting at the counter of the coffeeshop. I would like you to bring the story of this dress to the office!"

I stare at him. *What am I supposed to do?*

"Everything will be fine, just trust in yourself! Starting today, the red dress will be a symbol of listening for you!" Ed gets up and goes to the door. "See you!"

I examine the coffee cup in order to find the best way to start a conversation. *Nothing.* Doubts hit my self-esteem. *We will see*, I respond. I grab my cup of coffee and sit down next to the young woman.

"Hello!" I smile, and the woman, who has beautiful green eyes, also smiles at me.

"Hi!"

"You have fantastic dress!"

"Thank you," the girl blinks at the compliment, and suddenly it seems that there will be no obstacles to a conversation. The human world consists of things and the properties around them and listening makes this world more beautiful. "It's handmade!"

"Really? Can you tell you more?" I sit on the stool more comfortably, drink some coffee and listen for what she will tell me next.

Following Up

I have horizons that have to be conquered. KPI. The truth is, if I do not make phone calls, I do not have dates; if there are no dates, there are no deals; and if there are no deals, no goals are achieved. Where will I get customers? Ed? Ralph? Google? Acquaintances that I call in order to find out if any potential customer can be found among them? What am I'm going to present in my one-on-one session on Friday? I have a cup of espresso, and the hand holding it collapses on the table.

"Maggie!" Ralph runs into the kitchen. "Please, come to Pharaohs!"

"Why?" I raise my chin.

"I have a first meeting with the Femmet soap manufacturers! Join us and watch how things happen!"

I nod and stand up. I take my notebook from the sales office and arrive in the biggest Tamm meeting room. I see a woman with blonde hair and joy wrinkles around her eyes. She looks friendly and makes very good impression.

"Hello," I stretch out my hand, "I'm Maggie."

"Tamara!"

"I'm glad to meet you!" We shake hands.

Ralph joins us and closes Pharaohs' door.

"Tamara, this is my coworker, Maggie. She will also take part in the conversation." He sits next to the customer, places his laptop computer on the table and pushes it away from him. "Please accept Ed's apologies. His youngest child is in the hospital, and right now he must be with his family."

"I understand" she says, and I can see compassion in Tamara's eyes.

Amazing—with only one sentence, Ralph has created a relationship with Tamara. *Humility.* I open my notepad and write the title "Meeting" at the top of the page.

"From what I understood from Ed, he has written down some basic ideas about Tamm Solutions." A blank sheet and a pen are in front of Ralph. Why doesn't he use the computer? "In order to understand you better, please tell us what issues are currently causing the most difficulty in your work?"

I begin listening and finding out the customer's needs. How natural it all seems, now that I have learned about it! I laugh quietly to myself, and Ralph and Tamara do not even feel it.

"As you know, we are soap manufacturers, and we are both distributors and suppliers, and we have our own stores." Tamara is diplomatic. "At present, every customer is in their own database, but we have evolved to a level where they are no longer transparent. In my opinion, it takes too much time for project managers to deal with it!"

Ralph writes down some keywords on the sheet, almost without lowering his eyes and thus being in contact with Tamara all the time.

Don't start heading the wrong way, Maggie. Listen!

"I understand. When you say, 'too much time,' what do you mean by that?"

'To find the customer, write an invoice, and then make a report on the activities," Tamara specifies. "I have a feeling that everything is going slowly—" she is silent. Instead of asking a leading question, Ralph stays silent with her, allowing the representative of *Femmet* to deal with her thoughts and define the answer. "In this respect, Google calendar is quite inefficient. I can't see which project manager is dealing with a specific customer at any particular moment, and what is really going on there! It's a mess, I'd say. As a fast-growing company, we cannot afford to make mistakes! That would destroy our reputation. Our mission statement specifies that for us, reputation is one of the key elements of success!"

The more Tamara speaks, the more information she discloses. Ralph will be able to use this information later to pave the way to his customer's heart. I also want information. I want to understand the partnering conversation. I want to be calm and weighed, standing out with high listening and empathy skills. *That is how my Grandma sold flowers in the market many years ago. Now, it is transferred to me, working at Tamm. I am flying away again! Maggie, listen!*

"Thank you. How much time does it take for a project manager to complete this job?" asks my coworker. Tamara admits that sometimes it takes almost half a day, and it also lowers productivity.

"I understand." Ralph adds, "You shouldn't have to worry about the database, and millions of spreadsheet tables disappearing into Google Drive. Your time is better spent on planning how to conquer international markets and strengthening Femmet's reputation!"

"Yes, that's what we want! What do you have to offer?" The eyes of the Femmet lady shine.

 "Let's see how the system looks in reality." Ralph offers his story, including time management, business protection and project management already fixed in the value map. "I think we can find the most suitable solution for Femmet's situation."

A moment later I notice that the computer has not opened the demo version, and my coworker tightens lips. *What will happen?* If there is no demo, of course, it is not the world's biggest problem, but it can ruin a good sales moment. I sit quietly, not wanting to create additional tension in the room.

"What is your price?" Tamara changes the course of the conversation.

"The system is being updated right now. The demo will not be able to show insight, but this is my work surface!" Ralph is not worried about the failure of technology and turns on his profile. His extemporizing mind is welcome. He outlines Tamm's pricing and archly enrolls the calendar, tasks and data protection system in his story, thus taking over from Tamara. *Now do you understand? When needs have been recognized and solutions outlined, the customer can understand the importance of the functions as well!*

"How many people—users of the system—are we are talking about?"

"Four. Me and three project managers. Tell me, do you have experience dealing with soap manufacturers? What is the history of Tamm Solutions?" Tamara suddenly becomes skeptical and looks for holes in Ralph's story. I perk up and listen intently.

"*Senvo* is also one of our customers." Not one of Ralph's muscles moves. "I can put a special note on your file, to let my coworker who worked with Senvo become your project manager."

"Yes, that would be great!"

"As for us, we constantly evolve. We are a Canadian company and have had an office in New York for four years, and this year we opened a branch in England! Tamm Solutions was formed to help businesses take care of their business. We realized how important it is for businesses to have full knowledge and control of what is going on, to increase their profits and growth, and to reduce business risks to a minimum. These issues are also on our agenda, so we understand you perfectly. We have accumulated excellent experience and are able to help you!" Mr. Unbearable suppresses any possible doubt. This is a beautiful definition of Tamm though, and I quickly record it in my notebook, so I can use it on my dates as well.

Tamara smiles, but does not give us a final answer yet. It turns out that she is Femmet's sales manager and is likely to be among the people who will decide whether to purchase the Tamm software. Tamara and Ralph agree on the next steps of cooperation, and we all say goodbye. My colleague escorts Tamara to the elevator, while I remain sitting in Pharaohs, feeling very glad that I have learned about the difference the value map and listening. *It really works!*

"Maggie, if I didn't know you, you would seem to shine," laughs Ralph. He stands on the doorstep, with his hands in the pockets of his trousers. Instantly I recognize his sarcasm, and wink.

"Will there will be a deal?"

'We'll see. There is potential!" he states. "Please, book a session with me at two o'clock. We'll discuss how to conduct our meetings and how to behave during them. You will have to know that for your next date!"

I lift my thumb up, communicating that I am glad about our session, although I become more and more depressed. I know that on Friday there will be an assessment of my progress, and the situation with my KPI is pretty dismal.

How can I survive in Tamm if I don't know how to do the most basic things?

***

I clear my mind and wonder, *where could my next customers come from?* At the moment I cannot wait for Ed or Ralph to throw me a line, so I have to arm myself with enormous strength and wisdom. *A comfort zone is the most beautiful place— where nothing grows.* I stare at the poster on the wall. *What should I do?* I drum my fingertips on the table and try to hypnotize the phone, hoping that it will suddenly call by itself. Nothing happens. Magic apparently cannot overcome hopelessness. I get up to go for a coffee, but suddenly the computer screen flashes a new notification. It's a letter from one of my friend's friends who might be interested in Tamm. *Magic works! It still works!* I have a hope, and I have a way to achieve my KPI! I smile and register the contact information in the system. *So far, only one. No, at least one! The chain will begin to work, and there will be even more!* It is two o'clock, and I go to Vizier with a new dose of self-confidence. Ralph is still talking on the phone, but motions for me to sit down.

"Yes, Tamara, yes, I understand." Ralph is speaking with the Femmet lady and smiling widely.

No! He already has another deal? Come on, Maggie!

I look at my fingers, then open my notebook, to make it appear that I have something to do.

"Can I ask you for a reference to other companies where Tamm Solutions could be useful?"

Mmm, what? I frown. *Tamara will not take our CRM? Even after getting the full treatment from Mr. Unbearable?* As my coworker writes down three names and phone numbers, I recall what he said about the denials.

"Either you win, or you learn," he said.

"It sounds great, Tamara! Till our next call, then!" He drops the phone on the table and shrugs. "There will not be a contract. It happens!"

"Why?"

"One of the major shareholders is the co-owner of Verrit CRM. As you know, Verrit is our direct competitor. We were vetoed, despite the fact that Femmet is not going to use Verrit. We cannot do anything yet, we are powerless in because of this circumstance. We cannot influence that."

"Yeah, right! Didn't she know that?"

"It doesn't matter anymore, Maggie!" Ralph taps on the table. "What it is important is that lost customers can be also useful! When they give us negative news, we can ask for references. The customer feels guilty and will be happy to share their information. So, we can find a benefit even from a refusal!"

I can't believe it. *Does Ralph ever stop selling?*

"However, I am glad that you were here and saw how the conversation should take place!" He changes the subject.

"Yes, it was helpful," I admit. The Femmet refusal, coming after the Dolet Steel fiasco, is the second that I have been privileged to experience while working with the best salesperson at Tamm. I still cannot believe that something like that is possible!

"Do you have any questions after the date this morning?"

I open the page titled "Meeting" that I have supplemented during the day and show it to Ralph.

"Not bad, Maggie." Ralph tips his head in recognition. "What are you going to tell?"

"I believe that the meeting is a moment when the value card experiences a culmination. I would say that the meeting is surrounded by three large circles. The first thing we do is to allow the customer to discover their pain. Mainly because he has to come to the conclusion that they want to change something, to make the operations become more efficient! If we can, we give a promise about our software's effectiveness for the customer to accept, or—as demonstrated by Tamara—dismiss. This is followed by adapting our software to the customer's needs... because he is interested only that!"

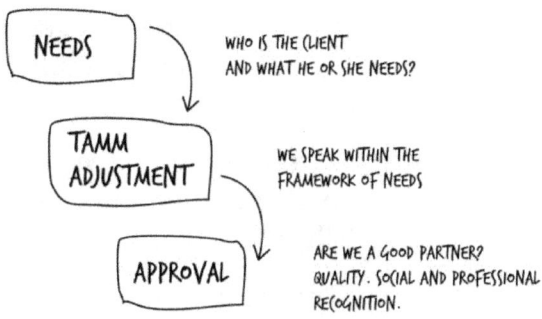

NEEDS — WHO IS THE CLIENT AND WHAT HE OR SHE NEEDS?

TAMM ADJUSTMENT — WE SPEAK WITHIN THE FRAMEWORK OF NEEDS

APPROVAL — ARE WE A GOOD PARTNER? QUALITY. SOCIAL AND PROFESSIONAL RECOGNITION.

"What does 'the approval' mean?"

"Oddly, what I observed with Tamara was the need for social and professional confirmation. Not only about our product, but about who we are—our people, our vision. Did you hear what she asked about the experience and history of Tamm Solutions? After the date I searched for the company you mentioned, Senvo, and soap manufacturers. It makes us seem experienced. We have already been recognized in the industry, and the customer likes that!"

Ralph inclines his head one more time. *This is too much for him,* I giggle in my thoughts.

"Leave the structure of the conversation! Now tell me what else have you noticed!"

"What else?" I run my fingers through my hair. "You got out of the situation with the computer well. The demo version did not work!"

"Yes, some virus has got into my system. Improvisation is useful! And serves us very often."

"By the way, I noticed that you did not use your computer, only a sheet of paper. Why?"

"The computer is meant for demonstration—entertainment. Nothing else! There are many programs in a computer that can distract your and your customer's attention, and you don't need that! Also, you should remember that prior to a date Skype, Facebook, Slack or any other program that shows notifications must be turned off! During a date, the computer should be placed away from you, and is used only when you have to highlight a visual image. Your phone should also be placed with the screen downwards in order not to disturb you. It is enough if you just have a white sheet of paper and a pen."

I sit on a chair and think about what Ralph just told me.

"And sit up with your back straight! Sit straight up to remind the customer what a serious and grounded person you are. Don't sit bent over, or slouch."

The computer is only for demonstration, and entertainment, I repeat in my head.

Sit with your back straight. I will work harder. Everything will be ok! I smile. Maggie, stand up! You can do it!

***

The session with Ralph has cheered me up. I look at the profile case, the posters about the comfort zone and sales calls, and my adrenaline is running over again. My fear of not achieving the KPI returns though, and I don't know what to think about that. One part of me reminds me that success is not eternal; the other part of me simply fills in the calendar on the *Tamm* system and is happy.

Shortly after the end of the business day, I receive a new e-mail. It is from Oliver Fallon from Metals LLC. With trembling fingers, I click on it, although my anxiety suggests leaving the traumatic news for tomorrow. *Why I do I presume it will be negative news?* I decide to take a chance and open it now.

Hello Maggie,

Thank you for your offer to meet for lunch and talk about the Tamm software in person. I gladly accept. Is this Thursday a good day for you?

Kind regards,

Oliver

YES! I GOT IT! If I could, I would do a somersault. YES! I HAVE A MEETING WITH OLIVER FALLON! I raise my fists over my head, cheering this good news. It is a pity that none of the other salespeople are in the office—I would shout to them in excitement, embrace them tightly and perhaps even give them a kiss. Oliver Fallon is my gold nugget, a prospective customer acquired on my own, and it makes the outside world shine like a Christmas tree. My ego bathes in pride, and I let it enjoy the first few minutes of my fame.

The Smart Customer

This morning's meeting is conducted by Ralph because Ed is still with his family. Meanwhile, Carl has a meeting with a customer, so I discuss yesterday's good news with Anna.

"There will be a deal!" My coworker finishes her narration on a beautiful note, while Ralph recommends that *"I walk away from the deal"*, if the customer does not say *yes* after a week. By the way, the green frog is now standing on Anna's desk. "We are not the customers' bellboys. We also have priorities! Let's learn that! Thank you, Anna. Maggie?"

"Tomorrow I have an appointment with Oliver Fallon from Metals, LLC!"

"Oh, congratulations, Maggie! It looks like you still have a chance to climb to the heights of Tamm!"

"Do I hear a compliment?"

'Don't dream too much," he grins. "If you meet the KPI, there will be a compliment for that."

I mutter to myself, *Mr. Unbearable likes to remind me of my place.*

"I know Fallon very well. He will be a hard nut to crack."

"Why do you say that?"

"Haven't you discovered this during your research?" my coworker teases, and I hiss at him. "Oliver Fallon is a monster of CRM!"

"In what way?"

"We call people like Fallon 'Smart Customers.' It means that they are smarter than we are. After checking almost all the major CRM systems available on the market, Fallon is unsurpassed in this field! I met with him two years ago, when tried to sell him our system—unsuccessfully. His knowledge was so extensive that what I was able to offer sounded like an apple puree for babies! At that time, he went to one of our competitors."

Oh no! Why do I always get the extreme customers?

"The fact that Fallon agreed to meet with you shows that he is open to change. Therefore, you must prepare for many questions and complaints from this customer. Prepare very well! Let's talk about it later. If you're lucky, you'll get really large customer, Maggie."

"What should I keep in mind?" I ask.

"Smart Customers are fans of your product. If you dazzle them, you will have a loyal follower. If not, then you will wait a long time for the next opportunity—as experience shows, at least two years!"

My brain switches into alarm mode. *Where should I start? Do I need to start reading Tamm's software documentation? Should I talk with the programmers about the greatest achievements and disadvantages of the program? But I can't do all that in one day! No. Yes? Maybe?*

I feel paralyzed. *What should I do?*

"Don't worry." Ralph tries to calm me down from somewhere off in the distance. "We just need to be prepared for everything!"

Be prepared for everything. How can I do that? I have to get a hold of my panic and drive it away. Maybe I have to shout and release my fear. Why do I get these customers?

***

I cannot stop thinking about Oliver Fallon.

Metals LLC is a large company, and I would be very happy if my first deal is with them, but I have no idea how to make a good impression on Fallon. I must be cautious—mistakes will cost us dearly. I am like a young racehorse, for whom a meeting with Fallon is like being evaluated by a buyer. Either I will be recognized as a professional or be sent back to become a work horse in the countryside. And then I'll never earn a good reputation!

"Maggie, don't daydream!" Ralph snaps his fingers in front to my eyes. "Focus, please! If you want to get Fallon, you have to show him a masterful performance!"

Surprised, I raise my chin a little. Looking out the window, I can see across the courtyard, where both of us enjoy eating lunch. *I need to learn how to handle objections.* But the sun is shining, and I'd rather bask in its happy warmth than force my mind to remember what most likely cannot be done.

"I understand how he communicates," my coworker says. "We will do this properly."

However, I know that this Smart Customer will not fit any date scenario invented by Tamm Solutions and its sales team, and Fallon will be the next customer to show me the door.

Ralph does not seem to share my premonition, and the feeling that we are going to fall off the cliff and—insanely—that we are the ones who will push ourselves off, becomes more and more depressing every second.

The meeting ends, and as we walk down the hall towards the kitchen, he tells me, "Objections are always connected to the fact that the customer does not see the value of the product and does not understand why they need it. Our job is to ensure that Fallon does not have such objections!" He reaches into the fridge and pulls out a box of takeout food, then puts a piece of sushi into his mouth. Ralph is a fan of Asian food. I have never seen him eating anything else. Giving in to his pressure, I have brought noodles with chicken in a spicy Chinese sauce.

"Can we counter all the customer's objections?"

"Let's try! What would you answer if Fallon says, 'there's no mobile application?'"

"Why we don't we have a mobile application?" I wrinkle my nose. "I don't know how to answer that!"

"You could ask him why this needs it, or for what purposes he intends to use it," Ralph tells me. "Very often people want to have an application on their phone because it's the fashion to do everything on their phone—without even realizing how vulnerable that may be. Our software stores very sensitive information, so we care about having the highest level of data protection. What happens if a phone is lost or stolen? Therefore, we do not have a mobile application."

"Do complaints arise because a customer wants to have the product? Or does not want it?"

"There are different situations, Maggie. When you're on a date and the customer begins to raise objections, you will know if the customer is ready to buy the product or not." Ralph eats the last piece of sushi.

"Can the customer complain about anything?"

"Oh, yes! Entrepreneurs will *always* find something to argue about, or bargain on the price. That is their nature. They have no money, it's too expensive, it's not the right time, they had a bad experience with another CRM, they only believe in a certain product; they may even say we have not offered what they need. There are many opportunities, you should only choose one!"

"Will you help me to deal with it tomorrow?"

"Of course, but you will have to learn to do it on your own!" He drinks his coffee.

"What would you say if Fallon wants to have a free system?"

"We don't give our software away for free, do we? Don't give it away! What is the basis of this objection?" My coworker looks at my face, as if he is searching for something.

"He won't spend money to invest in his company's growth?"

"What other reasons? Focus!"

"Sorry." I give in. *I have to make a choice: to believe in Ralph's experience, or to go a different way. How should I handle this? I have only a few hours to become the person offering the solution Oliver Fallon needs. A simple and easy answer is hiding here. What is it?* "I will say that other systems have worse technical support!"

"Don't say that! We never say bad things about our competitors. They are great!"

I am suspicious of this, but I choose to work with Ralph's suggestion. "Ok. Instead, I would say that we have excellent technical support, staffed by experienced professionals. I will offer to pay him if he can show me at least one other system that takes such excellent care of their customers."

Mr. Unbearable laughs.

"I'm serious, Ralph! We are charged with finding a solution, and the team stands behind us is constantly working to keep each customer satisfied, not only with our software as a product, but also with the customer's growth, since they are now working with Tamm Solutions. If they are not willing to invest in better time and resource management, as well as business intelligence, we really don't need to talk to them about it!

"Very well, Maggie, you just sold *Tamm*!" Ralph smiles. *Is he proud of me?* I smile in return, but my doubt does not diminish. Something in our strategy to acquire Fallon as a customer will definitely go wrong.

***

I cannot leave my work at the office; this is another evening when I take the job home with me. After an hour of lying on the couch, I have a feeling that I have analyzed the situation with Fallon incorrectly. I recite some inspirational phrases in my mind, trying to open some channel of creativity inside myself, but in vain. My worries lead to quite a dialogue in my mind.
What is not correct in my analysis? Why is it not correct? What questions do I need to ask? How do I ask them? I wish that I had been trained on how to handle objections. Then it would be much easier.

So, what are you worried about? I ask myself, throwing my fear and my courage into the same pot and asking for help. I hope it works. *What you worried about, Maggie?*

The meeting tomorrow, that's all! This meeting with Fallon could ruin me!

So, what can you do?

I must finalize the story! I must find the answers to every objection he could possibly have. And, I must listen.

What else can you do?

What else? I will definitely find out what Fallon needs, but the critical part will be how I handle his questions. I will have to know the answers. How can I be smarter? If I make any mistakes, any at all, this deal will be thrown in the garbage. And why does Ralph want to throw me into the heart of the battle and give me only a small knife as a weapon?

What does that mean?

There must be another approach. I am convinced of it! I need to have total control of the situation. I need to ask questions! No! Each time Fallon asks a question, I will answer it with a counter question! Go to devil!

Feeling drained, I quit this internal conversation and go into the kitchen. It feels good to concentrate on making a pot of coffee. I lean against the kitchen table. *Wrong analysis.*

Wrong? Think! What do I have to do?

Focus on ensuring that Fallon doesn't grind me into the floor under his foot!

How can you do that, Maggie?

It is a very long night, indeed.

***

We meet Oliver Fallon at his favorite restaurant, which specializes in Asian dishes. He is an elegant and sedate man around forty and instantly creates a professional and mythical aura around himself. While we wait for the food, we exchange formalities and compliments. I am tense. Despite the time that I have had to prepare for this meeting, I have still not decided how to attract this Smart Client to Tamm.

"What about the deal with Germany?" Ralph is curious. Yesterday we noticed in the news that Metals LLC was thinking of entering the Central European market.

"It's too early to tell," says Fallon. "It depends on many conditions! If we can convince potential partners about the quality, we have to offer them, the door to the German-speaking market will finally open for us."

"That's great! Good luck!" Ralph smiles.

Our order arrives. Fallon and Ralph have rice with vegetables, and I have some Thai soup. Ralph looks at me, indicating that I can start. I give him a small nod.

"Tell me, Mr. Fallon, what CRM system are you using right now?" I ask and drink some water to calm my nerves. I'm glad to be sitting down; otherwise, I'd already have lost consciousness.

"CRM Mainland. They're a good American company, and the software offers the basic functions that we need."

"Yes, I'm familiar with them! CRM Mainland has the potential...to compete with Tamm Solutions." I smile. *I can do this. I read the specifics about CRM Mainland yesterday.* "They have an excellent technical staff, but they still need to achieve the user friendliness that we have. That's one of our advantages." *I was afraid, but I'm no longer afraid.*

"I did not know that *Tamm Solutions* could surprise me!"

Laying the spoon on the edge of the bowl, I lower one hand to my side and cross my fingers. I am biting my tongue and thinking. *How can I win?* Shuffling on the seat, I pray for help, and then a furious dialogue begins in my mind.

Think!

How can I ask him questions in a way that avoids counter questions? How can I eliminate his technical questions?

I don't know! It's a dead end!

I don't understand the point of asking questions if none of us wins. Is it just to say something new?

I am looking at Fallon, and suddenly enlightenment comes. *I HAVE AN IDEA!*

"Never make the customer feel guilty about knowing too much or too little," Ed told me once. "No matter what questions we ask, we won't have all the answers."

We will not have all the answers! But at least asking questions will allow us to build new knowledge. The elixir of my victory will not come from asking the questions, but from listening to the customer's answers!

Oh god, what's happening to me? This is so simple and ingenious! Insane and obvious! I laugh inside myself because this could make or break the deal. This is the greatest challenge I might have today. *Ralph will not like it, but I don't care. Do you understand*, I tell myself, my fingers trembling, *this is an opportunity to show that I have the talent of a real salesperson!*

"Mr. Fallon, everything depends on whether you are ready accept Tamm Solutions' surprises!"

I take a breath. It's now or never. *Improvise! Take the initiative! Take risks!*

I can do it. Fear struggles with my other feelings and tries to convince that if I do this, I will betray my team. *Shut up! I was afraid but am afraid no longer.*

"I would be very proud if Metals LLC become our customer—mainly because along with you, we can top off your product to perfection!"

"In what respect?" Fallon is completely focused on me.

"I have to admit, most likely I will never be as smart as you about CRM products. The knowledge you have is like gold. You understand not only metalworking operations, which, incidentally, I think is a very fascinating industry, and also you have considerable knowledge of customer management systems and the light and dark sides of them."

I have put my spontaneous plan in action and try to kill Fallon's potential questions and objections about the specifics of your software. Inside, I am shaking, but adrenaline apparently hides it. *If I say that I cannot compete with his knowledge, will Fallon be ashamed to reproach me, if I am able to answer any of his questions?* I can do it. I have the motivation, and I cannot stop now.

I look at Ralph. He is pale.

"I would be happy to work with you and learn from you!" I lower my eyes and raise them up again. "Tell me, Mr. Fallon, what can I do for you to make the work of Metals LLC even better?"

Oliver Fallon is surprised. I can see it in his motionless face. Strictly—this time more than ever—I rein myself in. My brain starts to hurt.

"I am an idealist. I want my company to be the best. Whatever system I look at, and try, none of them offer what I need. Do you know what is really strange? If you take all the CRM systems together and add a few of my ideas, that would be perfect the CRM! Sometimes I feel that I have to hire programmers to make what I need!" Fallon reveals. "What can I expect from you, Maggie?"

"I propose to be your representative in Tamm Solutions! As a VIP customer, that will give you access to the updates faster than other companies on the market and personal invitations to test the beta versions and express your opinion. In addition, as your representative I will make care that your technical problems are resolved in a timely manner, without causing undue burdens to your business! I would like to become your authorized liaison person, and work with you to create a version of Tamm Solutions' CRM software that suits both of our business development goals!"

I am full of emotions, but I cannot allow them to show. *I cannot betray myself in front of pragmatic Ralph and the Smart Customer, Fallon. My humility has to work! To approach the situation from the other side—yes! I have jumped out without a parachute into the unknown, and I love it!*

Inscoffeed of victory, I receive a chilling silence. It seems so cold and inhospitable—as if somebody has switched off my hearing. Fallon blinks his eyes, and his gaze is like a vacuum cleaner that sucks the life out of me.

Ralph, what happened? How did this idea go wrong?

"What Maggie told you about is our special customer service program." My coworker, sensing my weakness, takes over the conversation.

I want to cry. *What did I do wrong?*

"We invite our most experienced customers to join us as advisors on product development, and depending on the budget available to upgrade it, supplementing our CRM with our customer's ideas." Ralph pauses. "This reduces business risks and promotes growth. This way, you would be able to influence *Tamm Solutions' CRM* in the future. Also, I have a feeling that you know

which ideas should be implemented first."
Ralph smiles.

Meanwhile, I am sitting still and staying silent. *How could I live with another failure if I cannot conclude the deal? To hell with learning and becoming reconciled to hearing "no!"*

"This program is labor-consuming, and for it to begin successfully, I have to provide information to our company management. Does this program comply with the goals of Metals LLC, and do you have sufficient funds available?"

"What amount of money we are talking about?" Fallon asks, looking at Ralph.

"The program participation fee is one hundred thousand dollars. Would your annual budget support such an investment?"

I can't believe it! *One hundred thousand for the deal, which normally costs five thousand? And since when do we have this Advisor program?* Tears appear in my eyes and I feel dizzy. *How far Ralph is willing to go in order to humiliate me? Please! PLEASE! Why is this happening to me? Run away! Ralph has pulled the rug out from underneath my feet, and I am falling. Why?*

"Can I think about it?" Fallon drinks some water. My colleague nods.

The head of Metals LLC is silent and starts to eat his lunch. We follow his example. We do not mention the offer, however, a discussion about challenges in the metalworking industry continues at full speed between Fallon and Ralph. I go to the washroom to regain my strength and gather my thoughts. When I return, my face is decorated with a wide smile, although I feel betrayed. The meeting lasts for another half hour. Finally, we are saying goodbye. I am a professional and promise to call to the phone number printed on Fallon's business card to find out his final decision. When Fallon leaves us, on the street next to the restaurant, I am completely drained of energy. There is nothing in me to propel me further. It hurts.

"How did you do that, Maggie?" Ralph's face is overcast, and it makes me feel even worse. I do not have an answer. "Your skill in getting out of that situation! It was almost amazing!"

What?

Raising my eyes, I realize that my coworker is not depressed, but confused. It takes ten seconds before he has recovers. Then Ralph laughs and starts to walk forward. *I do not understand anything!*

"I have not seen such respect for the potential customer before! It's a good way of thinking, Maggie, flattering him in order to build his ego! The only drawback is that you wanted to sell the Eiffel Tower again!"

"What do you mean?" I'm confused. "Ralph, tell me!"

"What is the law of the value map? 'Forget about the functions!' You found such a creative approach to Fallon, but you spoiled it with stories about what updates we will give and what technical support we will provide! Those was not the priorities for him! He only cares about getting his ideas implemented—his ideal version of the software!"

"But..."

"And from my experience, idealists will pay a lot in order to have what they want!"

I laugh, and it gets louder with every moment. Tiredness slides into the background, and I can. *I did not do anything wrong, I did everything almost right!*

"Let's keep our fingers crossed, and hope that your approach will be successful. Come on, I need some sushi. The food there isn't edible!"

Everything is ok. My mood lightens even more, and it feels like I'm sitting on a cloud and having fun.

"Let's go." I walk beside Ralph, feeling that I have faced a very difficult test and am proud of my efforts.

Oh, Maggie! The value map. Challenges.
Solutions. Remember!

***

I am back in Aquarius, making more cold
calls, when Anna rushes in.

"You have a phone call, Maggie. It's Oliver
Fallon!"

I run back to my desk thinking, *"He is*
calling me! What will he say?" I'm
nervous and excited at the same time. I
take a breath and try to sound calm and
professional. "Hello, Mr. Fallon."

It turns out that he has been looking for
someone who will advocate for his
interests in a CRM company. And, *he*
wants a long-term contract!

"I'm obsessed with finding the ideal CRM
system," he repeats, breathing into the
receiver, "and I'm willing pay to get it
faster than my competitors."

Mr. Unbearable was right—Fallon will pay
a lot to get what he wants. But more
important to me, this will be my first deal!

We agree on the day and time to sign the
contract and end the conversation. I sit
still for a moment on the edge of my desk
and let myself believe that it has

happened. I am filled with such strong, excited feelings that I have no words to describe it. *You're on a roll*, I praise myself. I've been trying for so long to make this happen. Trying, in an office full of sales professionals. Trying hard, in an environment that did not censure what I did. Working hard, with training and support from Ed and Ralph, and not being censured by Carl and Anna.

Finally, I will be able to prove Erica and my mother that I have the talent to succeed as a professional salesperson.

The outside world exists no more.

Slowly, I turn to look around the room. And then my gaze stops. On the bookshelf, the sales bell sits, shining with unprecedented beauty. I stand up and slide towards it. I stand up and glide towards it—grip the handle—and sound flows through my fingers, upwards and outwards all sides until it hits my brain and turns into a special salute. *I'm Maggie Kent. Salesperson! I'm a part of the gear of this team now.*

"Maggie?"

Ralph disturbs my thoughts, but I am glowing, radiant with happiness.

"Do you have a deal?"

I nod, and applause joins to the beauty of the bell's sound, and it makes me feel like a rock star. *This is my victory song! It tempts me to go on. More! I want more such calls. I want adrenaline to drive me constantly to the Mount Everest of sales.*

"Congratulations!" Even Ralph is applauding me. I am so proud, and relieved. "That's very good! When will you have your next deal?"

What deal? What is he talking about? I pinch myself and watch as he returns to his own work, as if my success means nothing. *Ok!* I return to my desk, sit down, and with a lazy movement transfer the Metals LLC card to a section that did not exist—until now. *Deals!* Now, it will be all right. *Nobody will stop me now!*

The Girl with A Lantern

The joy of concluding my first deal continues for the whole working week. I have chained myself to this emotion and won't let go. I have built my own pier. I've overcome its rough, rugged stage, and the road looks smooth and easy to walk on again. I have a lot to give to this world, and I will!

I open large door and walk out on the spacious rooftop terrace, which offers wonderful views over the rooftops of New York on Friday morning. There is a small coffee bar with soft chairs and a sculpture gallery. I do not understand yet why I am here, but I'm glad to here. I have not seen this view before, and it stimulates my thoughts. I find Ed sitting at a table next to the sculpture of a girl with a lantern in her hands.

Ed waves to me.

"Hello, Maggie!" He points to the other chair at his table. "Was it easy for you to find me?"

"Yes!"

"How are you doing after the deal with Fallon?"

Great, I would like to shout, but I restrain myself.

"Very well!" I reply, a little cautiously.

"I have already ordered coffee for both of us."

"Thank you! I will enjoy it!" I ease into a wicker chair and put my handbag by my feet. "This is beautiful! What is this place?"

"We are in a rooftop Sculpture garden. It has just been opened by my friends, and the official opening is in a week."

"So, this is brand new?" I look around. "It's beautiful!"

"Yes, everything is ready," Ed tells me. "Currently, Sculpture, as they call themselves, is an inspirational group for artists that has been hidden from the public. There is a secret cafe for artists and art students; they can exhibit their work here and get feedback from the other artists. This is not the best business development opportunity, but the community that stands behind them is considerable!"

Ed's words make Sculpture sound like a small miracle, and it makes me feel special to be here. Being invited was a unique and exclusive offer—exactly the same as I suggested to Fallon. *We offered it together, Ralph and me.*

"I have invited you here to tell you a story. Since you have acquired the ability to listen, and the example of working with Fallon shows that you have mastered it very well, I think that you will be able to understand the essence of this story!"

I nod. My experience tells me that such stories are always followed by a test, and this test might be about asking questions. *Listen!*

"Once I met the artist who created this sculpture." Lewis points to the girl with lantern. "A very interesting lady, who has earned her Fine Arts degree in at age sixty-five. I wanted to know the girl's story and asked about it.

"The girl was a lantern master, and the best in her village. When one of craftsmen from the neighboring village found out about her, he decided to visit her and express his admiration. The journey lasted for several days. When the craftsman finally came to see her, he said, "I see that your trade flourishes. I've never seen so many beautiful lanterns anywhere else! Don't you want people everywhere to talk about you?"

And she answered, "I would like that!"

He continued, "I see the way that you are living, although you earn a lot of money. Don't you want to invest in the development of lanterns, to hire new masters and become even richer?"

She answered, "I would like to!"

He continued: "Why don't you do it?"

And she replied: "I do not need it! I am not making lanterns. I let you and everyone else to make the light in the dark. I am sorry that I could not see where you were going, and it cost my time and your money. Unlike you, I cannot change this darkness!" It turned out that the girl was blind, but the craftsman had not noticed that. He left feeling ashamed, but later became an even greater admirer of this girl!"

Ed finishes the story, but I still look at the sculpture. It seems to be different now. Not modest and simple, but rather spiritual and noble.

"Do you realize what the admirer did wrong?"

"He did not listen!" I cross my fingers. "He asked only what he had taken to be the truth and did not try to understand what was important to her! He went to her with a full set of assumptions, and it probably cost him a deal!"

"That's right! He pointed out that he sees, but in fact he did not see and did not hear anything. Listening goes hand in hand with asking questions, and that is the topic I want to talk about with you today."

Yes, I was right! And I am ready to absorb new knowledge. I do not want Ralph to have to save me from any more awkward situations with a customer.

"What can you tell me about questions?"

I narrow my eyes, thinking about the answer. *Theory is always followed by some practical task.* I look around to find the victim Ed has chosen to strengthen my questioning skills. Nearby is a young man with a sketch pad in his hands, a lady with a little boy, and the barista.

"Maggie, where are you traveling to?"

"Nowhere!" I laugh and remind myself to concentrate. "These...questions allow us to clarify the customer's opinion. There are closed questions, most of which require a yes or no answer, and open questions, through which we learn how much the customer knows about the topic. We use questions to find out if we can be useful!"

"What do you like about questions?"

"Most of all?" I push my hair behind my left ear. "Oh, you'll love this, Ed! A question is a provocation, because every question also adds to our knowledge," I say, being very serious. "We give the customer the freedom to reply, however, we reserve the right to specify what they

have to speak about! How evil that
sounds!"

"Maggie, I am glad you are making
progress! Are you ready for the test?" The
boss takes a breath.

What? Of course! I am surprised that Ed
has warned me about it.

"Now, I will be in a meeting with Tom
Audrin, a patron of the arts, who has
expressed interest about *Tamm*. Your task
is to find out, with the help of questions,
how we can cooperate!"

I am concerned. *This is not a test but
dealing with a real customer. Why is Ed
asking me to do this? I'm not ready!*

"Do not forget what we talked about, and
what you heard!" says Lewis.

"Ok, I will try!" *Courage, please be with
me. Listen, and ask questions! You can do
it!*

***

Ten minutes later, a young man sits down
next to us. I hesitate. I bite my tongue.
Listen without prejudice, Maggie! The guy
is wearing sunglasses, and he looks very
neat.

"Have you already ordered?" asks Tom.

'Yes," says Ed. "The coffee is great! Like everything else here!"

What? Tom is the owner of Sculpture?

"Thank you! I'm happy to hear you say that!" Tom smiles.

He's not only a patron, but also a businessman. What does Ed think about this? Why exactly would Tom want our software? Why did Ed describe him as a patron of the arts when it would make sense to call him the owner of Sculpture? Why do I have so many questions?

"Maggie?" The boss disturbs my thoughts, and I am a little startled.

"Yes..." I lean forward. "Ed mentioned that you are interested in Tamm Solutions! Can you tell me more about yourself?"

"Yes!" Tom straightens his back and remembering Ralph's words about how to behave on a date with a customer, I follow his example. "Besides Sculpture I have The Patron's Foundation—I support young artists with scholarships, workshops and grants. The previous manager of the foundation created a small riot of activity reports, and the new manager needs to organize all these reports and extract the useful information for us. I want to introduce Tamm Solutions as one of the solutions!"

No! I left my laptop computer in the office! How will I show a demo version? Why didn't Ed tell me to bring the computer? This one situation when I have not foreseen all the possible circumstances. *I have forgotten that I can find potential customers anywhere. Stupid! Maggie, listen to the customer rather than yourself,* I remind to myself.

"What issues do we need to discuss?" I ask. It does not sound good. "What exactly creates the most difficulties for you?" I make a correction.

"Non-transparent communication with the artists who receive the foundation's resources! It is not clear when and how much money we transfer to them. Moreover, the reports submitted by artists—beneficiaries— are scattered over a million folders. When there's a dispute, we can't even to find the necessary information."

"Clearly," I say. *There will be a deal.*

"Tom, we'll leave you for a short while," Ed suddenly mutters. "I have to talk to Maggie."

What's going on? Why does Ed need to talk to me now, when we have a customer right here?

"I'll wait."

We sit at the coffee bar, and Lewis sighs.

"What can you tell me about the customer?"

"I think the *Tamm* software will be helpful for him!"

"Why?"

"There is a mess in The Patron's Foundation—they don't know where their money is going, or how much! We can solve that."

"Why do you think that Tamm is suitable for him—even if you have not asked the right questions?"

"What do you mean?" I am confused.

"Haven't you noticed?"

What? What I do I need to see? I look at Tom, who is being served a latte. He carefully gropes along the table until he finds the mug and picks up very carefully. Tom is blind, and I, like the craftsman in the story, did not notice it. *That's why Ed told me the story about the girl with the lantern.* I feel a tremendous sense of guilt.

"The more desperately you try to sell, the fewer sales you will make. I want to make you an excellent salesperson, not a mediocre one!" Ed is frustrated.

I am embarrassed, and when we return to the table with Tom, I do not know how to behave. I'm worried, and my fingers tremble. I cannot do this.

"Maggie, it would be useful for you to know how Tom established his foundation! It's a good story!" the boss helps me.

"You think so?" Tom asks. "Maggie, do you have any knowledge of the art world?"

"No!" I shake my head.

"I used to paint. I lived in Canada, where I managed to join the elite new artists and sell my works for good money. When I returned to New York, I fell in love with a third-generation sculptor. She didn't have enough money to pay the membership fee and show her work in a sculpture exhibition, so I offered to help her. It paid off. She received excellent reviews from the exhibition, and now many of those works are in private sculpture collections. Then I realized that despite the fact that I could not paint anymore, I could still be part of the art world—that I am able to help, and to do other things! Creating a foundation seemed to be the right choice for me, because it allows me *to get involved* the art each day.

"So, I have gone from a man who had his dream taken away from him and become a person to whom a stack of other dreams was given, and their value far exceeds what I had wanted in my life." The arts patron drinks his latte and puts it on the table.

"And the sculptor, who is the granddaughter of the creator of this lantern sculpture, I proudly now call my wife." He smiles impishly.

Sitting in the chair, I realize that my arms are sweaty. I become sentimental. *Maggie, concentrate! Why did Ed want me to hear this story? So that I once again I would break down and show my emotions?*

"Have you thought about how this non-transparent communication affects the work of your foundation? Exactly where it inconveniences you?"

A talented artist lost the opportunity to study in Milan because we didn't pay the admission fee in time. These mistakes prevent artists from realizing their potential!"

I cannot fight with such customer. I admire Tom.

"About how many artists we are talking about? How many people do you help per year?"

"From twenty to thirty per year, but I would like to help more! Although we are a non-governmental organization, we look forward to more growth."

What? Twenty deals per year? When the expression on Ed's face tells me that I have heard correctly, I finally realize the true reason why I am here— and it saddens me. Tom Audrins is not the kind of customer Tamm Solutions is looking for, and Lewis knew it from the very beginning. He is making me fight with myself. My job is to say "no" to Tom. How can I turn him down when he has such a passion for helping others?

Tom's foundation is not a business, I explain to myself. *It is a charity, and under no circumstances will it reach Metals LLC's level of success.* The only thing that the foundation needs is an intelligent person who knows how to work with computers, *a spreadsheet program*, and a free project management tool. The world of computer technology is full of such tools.

"Maggie?" Ed asks. "What do you think?"

What do I think?

"I told Tom that his foundation does not need our software, at least not now! To me it does not seem like a good long-term investment!" Ed states his position very clearly, making sure I will not misunderstand him.

I open my mouth to express my support notes for the boss, but I stop. *I want to have this deal. Another deal.* I am a hypocrite. Part of me is ready to take the craftsman's place and offer the lantern girl what she does not need. *I'm terrible!*

"Maggie, what do you recommend?"

If Tom buys our software it will cause only financial losses for the foundation, because the monthly subscription fee must be paid, regardless of the number of transactions. In a best-case scenario, Tom would only need our software for two contracts for the foundation per month, and that is an inappropriately small figure for our software product. In addition, Tom would have to make major expenditures in his foundation that don't actually help the artists. Where would he get the money, so it does not look like Tamm is bleeding him of his resources?

"I think we need to assess the contribution of our software to your foundation."

What contribution? What system? Here is a clear case where I should refuse to sell our software.

Disappointment runs through my whole body.

I want to help Tom as much as he helps others. Is that too much to ask?

So why I didn't I tell him the truth?

You either win or get a lesson?

Indeed!

***

Inside myself, l hear constant accusations of not living up to my moral principles, and it becomes intrusive. When I can no longer endure it, I go home. I need a glass of wine. After dinner I wrap myself in a blanket and sit on the sofa, to sum up my thoughts.

I know that Ed is disappointed in me. For the rest of the day, after the date with Tom, his paternal gaze expressed dismay about my actions, and I can't disagree with him. We even did not complete the training on questions as he told me that he did not have enough time. We did not even have our one-to-one session, and after this, it may not happen.

Meanwhile, Tom Audrins has announced that he will buy our software at any price, and now it is my duty is to bring the deal to the end. I was looking for excuses. It is not that I am forcing Tom to buy our product. That is his choice. I should not feel bad about the customers' needs, and the budget available to them!

True, my conscience takes over my mind like an incurable virus that wants to crush my towering ambitions. I struggle with the ethical dilemma inside me. I cannot believe that Tom would spend his money on our software instead of for the benefit of young artists. What is even worse, the foundation is Tom's most cherished idea, and I played with his feelings to satisfy *my* ego, my desire to have a second deal. What would my profile case say? What situation is this, fear or courage? All these doubts are the reason why I have not still rung the sales bell.

"Maggie, why are you sad?" Erica sits down next to me and puts her feet up on the coffee table.

"Work issues."

"Again! What happened this time?"

"Erica, you don't understand!"

"What should I understand? Tell me, Maggie."

I tell Erica the short version of my date with Tom, and she does not miss a word of the conversation. In the past, I had not noticed this talent. Erica has strong opinions and she changes them very rarely, but she always listens carefully to what other people say. How unusual!

"I don't understand what you are worried about."

"Erica!"

"When applied for this job, you told me that were going to do your utmost to achieve great results! You would not just be good in Tamm Solutions, you wanted to be the best!" My friend sighs. "Although I don't like it, you will have to climb over dead bodies to get to the top. Salespeople do that! You said that this guy...Ralph?

You said that he doesn't know anything about ethical standards. The most important thing is to conclude the deal! If you want to survive there, you must learn to be a carnivore, my friend! You have no choice."

"You're right!" I bow my head. I have to achieve my KPI, and there is no place for a heart in business. "Why didn't Ed tell me that?"

"Tell you what? That he is proud of you? Be glad that he does not immediately require you to sign the third deal!"

I laugh at that. I assume that he will ask for that on Monday during the meeting. I will prepare and be ready for all questions that he could ask me. I will be unbreakable! I need to believe that I will get through with the deal with Tom and all my future tasks, otherwise I will not succeed. I drink some more wine and sit deeper in the sofa. My friend hugs me and comforts me. I fall asleep right there.

***

There is a hole in the middle of my pier, and I have no idea how to get over it. There are lights at the end of the pier, and they are so beautiful that I want to touch them. But they are mine, aren't they? Unless I get over...who has destroyed the path along *my* pier? Who? I remain standing on one side of the concrete, feeling ashamed of my weakness. Who's holding me back?

***

I did not sleep much on the weekend, and on Monday I arrive at work shortly before eight o'clock. I am sleepy, and I hope that coffee will help. I am surprised to see that Ralph is already in the office. My colleague sits there, leaning back in his chair, reading a book called *Leader Without A Title* by Robin Sharma.

"Maggie!"

"Hi." I am trying to smile but fail. "Ralph?" I need to know that I am acting properly regarding the issue with Tom Audrins' foundation.

"Yes?"

"The Tom Audrins' deal. What do you think about that?"

"In what respect?" My coworker puts the book down and stands up. "As I understand it from Ed, everything is proceeding just fine."

"Yes, it is." I take my purse off my shoulder and go to my desk. Maybe it is not worth asking the question if the answer is already known.

"Maggie, what happened?"

"What am I supposed to do when a customer wants to buy our software, but it isn't right for him? Would you sell him our CRM?"

"No!" he answers sharply and dispassionately.

"Why not?" My knees are a little weak; I sit down and take a breath.

"These are not the ethical principles of Tamm Solutions! We do not work like that!" Ralph is categorical, and it destroys all my expectations. "Not everyone who is suitable to be our customer, *can* become our customer! Salespeople who only want to make sales, and don't care about the customers' well-being, are not welcome here!"

Sleep has disappeared, and I will not need coffee any more. *What have I done? I'm a toad—even worse than Mr. Unbearable. I've cast my faith on the fire, and it burns, laughing in my face.* I am afraid. *Tom Audrins is a failure that could cost me my job! Oh, my God!*

"Imagine a customer evaluation phase like in *Tinder!* We send the that we like to the right, and to the left, the ones we do not like! How are you going to select them? Evaluate how they look, find out if you have common friends and interests? *This boy has big muscles in the photo; he's showing off. No, I don't want him!* And so, you go through the offer and make a decision! You do not send everyone to the right, do you? Why would let all the customers go to the right?

"Then you arrange a date with one of those with whom you have a mutual sympathy. Why do you go on a date? To see how the guy looks... to make a decision again. Will you stay with a guy just because you have common interests, but no emotional and physical attraction? How long will you stay with such a guy? How long will you keep such a customer?"

"Aren't concluded deals and the money from them important resources on which Tamm depends?"

"The most important resource in Tamm is you," Ralph corrects, "and your skill to make the right decisions! We know what to call those who do not think about long-term liabilities and sell themselves for money! I do not want that to be on our business cards!"

"What should I do?" I whisper. *I've betrayed myself, Tom and Tamm Solutions, and now I understand why my pier has disappeared. How do I correct this? To whom do I say it? Ralph? Do I need to discover what I think?*

"Maggie?"

You either win or get the lesson. What happens to me now?

"What should I do?"

Ralph takes the keys and grabs my hand.

"Do you know?" I breathe, seeking to overcome my fear, which gradually takes away my ability to move. *Has Ed already said something to Ralph? Of course, he has!* I appreciate that my coworker isn't disgracing me, at least not openly. And not now.

"You already know what is most important. Shall we go?"

"Where?"

'To Sculptures!" says Ralph. "Small mistakes are quickly recognized and fixed! Mistakes that are concealed and from which we hide are much harder to correct. What will your next step be?"

I nod. Anything that can give me any ray of hope, I welcome with open arms.

Maggie, I say to myself, *it is right not to burden Tom with issues that don't belong to him.*

It turns out that questions bring not only knowledge about potential customers, but also about us; they help both the customer and us to understand if we need each other. For the first time, my greed has brought my common sense to its knees, and I promise myself that I will become better. Starting right now!

***

It's strange, but by the time I meet with Tom, I am in a security bubble. Ralph is standing next to me. He says that Tamm has reviewed the possibility of working with Tom's foundation again and does not see any further development possibilities. Mr. Unbearable is drastically direct, without caring about Tom's feelings. It brings peace to me. I mention that the foundation will benefit more by hiring a professional project manager who will be able to continue the foundation's growth scrupulously and creatively. Tom is not disappointed. I even get the impression that he was expecting such a turn in the negotiations, and that removes the burden from my soul.

"What did you learn?" Ralph asks when have left Sculptures.

"The customer is a person, not a cash machine. We salespeople are also people, not greedy monsters. We all—both customers and salespeople—are in charge of our conscience! I would never forgive myself for making this deal if it had been concluded!"

My colleague smiles. I am fascinated by his compassion. For the first time I see more in Ralph than the usual insensitivity, pursuit of perfection and top-class professionalism. Ralph cares about what happens to me and what kind of salesperson I will become. He also maintains that the coffee engine is never going to stop working.

My Place on the Team

Time seems to disappear quickly, and I am happy working at Tamm Solutions. Since the negotiations with Tom I have enjoyed more success and fulfilled my KPI. My efforts to find more customers starts to pay off, and Erica also helps me, despite her prejudice against sales. I began to appreciate my contribution to the company and craftsmanship being built from training. The end of the month approaches, and only eleven dates remain in order to reach my monthly quota.

Tamm Solutions is finally my home. I like my coworkers and our daily jokes. I am quite accustomed to all that is here, including the printer and the water machine that hums in the background and does not fall silent. I am even happy with my corner of the room, where the sun does not shine at any hour of the day. And the posters, which encourages me to violate my comfort zone or reminds that *the receiver is not an enemy*. There is Ralph, who I gradually began to rely on, and Ed, my mentor. *This is my place.*

***

Entering Ed's office for our one-on-one session, I find my boss standing at the window, deep in his thoughts. Smiling, I realize that even someone at the peak of professionalism, such as Ed Lewis may, look like person who is lost in another dimension. Does he get his confidence from there?

"Ed?" I ask, and my boss chief twitches.

"Hello, Maggie." He runs his fingers through his hair and sits down in his chair. I take a seat opposite him. "I was just thinking about you!"

I lift my eyebrows. *Why would he think about me?*

"How are you?" he asks.

"Great! I've been very productive in the last few days."

"That makes me happy! I want to commend you also for your good work in the *Tamm* system. Only few of our Tamm employees are so detailed regarding the data they input. How are you doing with your dates? Are they filling up?"

"It's moving forward. I'm very close to making my quota!"

"To whom have you sent out *follow-ups* after a date?" Lewis sits back in his chair and watches me.

A follow-up is a message that reminds the customer of you, I repeat in my head, as if Ed had asked an exam question. *Once the conversation has been started, we use them to get to the date. But after the date they summarize the main points of conversation so that both we and the customer have a clear vision of the next action steps.*

"I have sent them to everyone who expressed interest in further communication."

"What are you doing with the customers who say *no* at the date?" He squints, and I feel that it will be followed by something subversive. My heart trembles. I have done nothing with them and understand that that will not be a satisfactory answer. "Maggie?"

"Nothing. I have not written them anything."

"You're responsible to the customer for the time they have spent with you, and it's part of your job to write a summary of your meeting and thank them for their time! There have been cases—and in my experience it happens quite often—that when a customer receives such message, they have changed their mind and bought the Tamm software. Ralph was supposed to tell you this. Our biggest competitor is the answer, "we have not made a decision!"

I put up with the reproach. I don't think that it looks very significant compared to the rest of my work. Of the nine customer dates I have gone on this month, I have only heard "no" from five, and one of them was Mr. Customer, who I would not write to, even if I have to.

"Then please do so. When you finish that, write to the customers who refused as well!"

"Despite the fact that some time has passed?" I frown. *No, I do not want to write to Vincent!*

"Yes, Maggie! It seemed to me that you already got the lesson from working with Tom Audrins. You have to do enough to give the customer the impression that they have not been used, and seriously evaluated. When you communicate with a customer, you are the face of Tamm Solutions!"

I know! Vincent. I was just his daily entertainment. How can I flatter him after all this?

"Are you settled in?" Ed changes the subject, stating that he will not accept any deviations from my tasks. So, I will have to write to Raymond Vincent.

"Just today I recognized that I like it here a lot! I would like to figure out where to find more customers. I've reviewed all of the phone directory page, and now a kind of network is made up of contacts from my acquaintances, but I believe that there must be other options!"

"Well, I'll make a note of that." he looks mixed-up. What happened? "Maggie, I have thought about your future development in the company."

These words destroy my good mood in one second, and my heart fills up with a new wave of doubt.

"I have carefully followed-up your work, and I am happy with what I see!"

Can I expect good news? Ed's assessment would be like praising the President.

"Some things you do very well, some—not well enough. What worries me right now is your ability to cope with pressure."

I collapse.

"Tom Audrins proved that an unusual deal can knock you off the rails. It is hard for me to understand whether you will be able to cope with these customers, and whether you will be able to deal with large customers!"

I will be able to cope! Tom Audrins has also proved the I can mend and overcome troubling situations to avoid professional heartache in the future. Isn't that the essence of my potential?

"I've decided to give Oliver Fallon to Anna," the boss says, and becomes silent.

What? Did I hear that correctly? Fallon has been taken away from me? Why? Because of Tom? That is not fair! Why would he be given to Anna?

"I want you to understand that you should not take it personally. You did a great job in order to get Fallon in *Tamm*, but Anna's experience with VIP clients makes her more qualified for the subsequent steps. We hired her *specifically* to work with this type of customer."

Ed has torn away my achievement and it feels like he is sending me back to kindergarten. *What does he mean, "Anna is more qualified?" And how can I not take it personally? This is more than personal! He takes away the only deal I have made, and only because do not trust me? How can I trust him?*

"Ralph also agrees that first you need to understand the basics of sales and ethics in order to continue with challenging situations."

The boss is throwing arguments at me, but they all sound unreasonable. Now, this office seems too small, and confining. I do not want to be here!

"Of course, I encourage you to participate in all the dates together with Anna, so that you can learn and improve! You're still a part of the deal."

How convenient. I clench my hands. I have no desire to listen to Ed. *What part of the deal am I? I will not be Anna's secretary in the Fallon case! The whole team has spit on me, as if I am worthless; why don't they trust me? Does Ed really think that I will accept such conditions with my arms wide open? What really is the role of KPI, if the company treats my customers like a juggler— "this will be your deal, no, it will not be your deal." No. I am not going to work like this!*

I wait for the end and return to the salespeople's office, where Carl is going to conclude another deal. He is talking on the phone, already holding the sales bell in his hand, and I wonder if he has really won the deal. I sit down at my desk and hide in the computer. I will not look at the profile case, or my KPI, and certainly not do any follow-up letters. At this moment, Tamm does not seem important to me.

***

I spend the day in silence. I also choose to have my lunch alone, eating a Greek salad at the kitchen table, not joining my coworkers. I have fear and courage, I have passion and motivation, but I have no ideals anymore. Who is right—me, for dreaming about becoming a professional salesperson, or my mom and Erica? I want to believe that I am right.

When the computer clock shows six o'clock in the evening, I pick up my handbag and go home. Today I have no desire to stay in office any longer than the eight contractual working hours. Tomorrow will be a new day, and I hope that it will come with other adventures.

"Bye," Ralph says to me. "Till morning!"

I squint. His friendliness is really annoying. I didn't expect him to say anything. *I will not have enough strength to deal with large customers? We shall see!* Ralph is the one to be blamed for all this.

"Maggie, what happened?"

"Thank you for telling Ed to take away Fallon from me!" I say angrily.

"I didn't tell him to do that." He crosses his hands.

Who is a hypocrite now?

"Why did you do it? You saw what I did!"

"Maggie, you still have to learn! You will have a lot of customers like Fallon, whom you would win without any help!"

'What?" I step back. Is he trying to say that without his support, I would not have this deal?

"You're not in danger," Ralph mumbles, so dispassionately that it angers me to the depths of my heart.

"Endangered? You think I feel endangered? You are wrong!" I raise the tone of my voice. *Perhaps, however, I feel fear? Perhaps feeling threatened is what makes me so worried?*

Why is everything that happens so controversial? It hurts when every time I come out as a loser.

"Calm down!"

"Ralph, I cannot believe you! How can I work with you if you are evaluating by default, whether I will be able to do something? You have not even given me the opportunity to prove myself!"

"Your unhappiness proves that we made the right choice!"

"Screw you!" I mutter. *I can't talk to him.*

"Maggie!" suddenly I hear Ed's voice.

I turn around and feel stunned for a moment. I didn't expect this. My face becomes pale, and I take a breath. I am ashamed.

"Maggie, what has happened?" Ed asks. He is very calm. That makes me angry again – have they so simply, at a moment's whim, decided to stop me from working with Oliver Fallon?

"Ed, I do not like it when your judgement about whether I can do something or not is confirmed by Ralph!"

"Why would he do that?"

"Because he does not see my progress!"

"And who see your progress, Maggie?"

"I see it! You see it!"

"Do you think that's enough?"

Why Ed is trying to instill a sense of guilt in me? It will not work!

"I highly recommend you not to jump beyond the limits of your abilities!" The boss raises his eyebrows. "Remember that you are in a company that has worked well before your arrival. If you blame Ralph because I gave the deal with Fallon to Anna, by making such an accusation you highly exceed the level at which we allow team members to communicate!"

I am standing with my mouth open. *I still feel guilty. Why?*

"I told you that Anna has experience working with VIP clients. If you talk to her more often, you will understand what you can learn! I'm not your nanny, Maggie; it's not up to me to take care for you and fuss over you. You're a grown woman, not a teenager. Either you make up your mind to cooperate and be professional or find another place to work. I will not tolerate quarrels!"

I shiver. My fury turns into fear, wild fear. Fear of myself. Of the future. Of what Ed can do. Of what I have already done.

"Ralph will stay in his place. Let's see if you manage to stay in yours!" Ed is disappointed. Again. "Thank you. Have a nice evening!"

Ed Lewis goes away, leaving me in the middle of the sales office. Soon Ralph, Carl and Anna leave too.

I am left alone in the office with my truth. My outrage has turned into disappointment, and a sense of guilt. *Do I want to stay here after all?*

***

My pier has collapsed once again. The storm has destroyed it. Only ruins are left, appearing in the middle of the sea like an uninhabited artificial island that will batter the most inconsiderate ships against the underwater concrete. I am caught between the ruins and the land, between my lost dreams and truth. Now there is nothing but fighting and building all that again with my bare hands.

Fitting In

"The *Tamm Solutions* system is excellent," says a man with an extremely narrow chin. He sits heavily in a chair. "But it will take too much time for us to enter our data! I cannot impose such a burden on our employees. It looks too complicated…"

I narrow my eyes and take a breath, a deep, deep breath. *What would Ralph say? What would he do? He must be able to deal with three objections slipped into one sentence.* We are on a date, and Ralph sits opposite Bradley Nichols, a man with the same red hair as himself, and no doubt with the same character. The last half an hour, during which my coworker has pointed out Nichols' challenges in detail and the solution proposed by our Tamm Software, has been quite an interesting show with two self-assured individuals in the starring roles. This is one of benefits of a salesperson's life that I still have.

"We adapt *Tamm Solutions* to the specific needs of each customer and make it as simple and understandable to the customer as possible. This means that although the software looks complicated right now, your daily work will not be like this at all. Your system will have only those functions that are necessary for your work, and the other, unnecessary functions, will be removed so they will not trouble you. You will be the boss of your system!"

Ralph is invincible. He will not let his victim go while he can still be hunted down.

"In terms of data input, can I ask how much time it currently takes you to enter the information?"

"I will not be able to give you exact figures, but it's about five hours per week per employee, on average!"

"Where is the data you enter stored?"

"In a spreadsheet program! And Google Drive!"

"Great! What happens to the information when you hire new employees? What happens to the information when some of your employees leave?"

Nichols keeps silent. His temporal veins pulsate, and he looks surprised. I watch in amazement as the customer's chest rises in stress, and wonder what dilemmas are in his head. *The customer will always have objections, and it looks like Mr. Unbearable is the ideal candidate for overcoming them.* I have no doubt about that! *He will surround Nichols with his great self-esteem, frightening humility and knowledge, and will smash any doubts with a single shot.*

"Of course, you will need to enter data! We'll be with you during the transition period, to show how the system works; that is part of your investment, so you can work more productively! In the long-term, it means that your information always stays with your company! Absolutely all your data—who your customers are, what actions have been carried out regarding them, and all your communications! If an employee leaves, information does not have to leave with them; instead, it stays with you. When a new employee begins to work with you, they will not start from scratch. Instead, they will take over the customer management from the point where it stopped, and all the information still stays with your company. This way, you will avoid having holes in your operations, and avoid downtime. It enhances the security of your data and protects your business!"

Ralph has found Bradley's values and manages them in front of the customer like an excellent conductor. At the beginning of the date, Nichols looked distracted and did not see our software helping his business. Now he is a completely different person. In our offer, he sees a guarantee to overcome his major challenges. And Bradley says yes. Without hesitation. Immediately. As if rescuing the world from decline depends on his answer.

I smile. *Ralph's words are so simple!* You have to be able to find logical connections and use them for your benefit, with untold faith in every word that is pronounced. With the head held high, a strong voice and a confident look. Without any possibility that something could go wrong. I want to fight for the pier. For my rights in *Tamm*. For excellence. For Fallon. It is my destiny.

True, my enthusiasm fades as quickly as it appeared, when I remember my dispute with Ed and I just stood there, blankly blinking my eyes, unable to make up my mind. After Ed's threats, something has broken down in me. If I can understand what it is, I will fix it. If not, then...

***

Ralph rings a sales bell, announcing the deal with Bradley Nichols to the entire office. This time he is ringing it for longer than usual, and I go to the kitchen, so I won't have to pretend to be happy. For me, it has become cold and uncomfortable in the sales office, and when it is filled with the sound of the sales bell ringing, I am ready to laugh at anyone for hypocrisy. "Tamm sales team" is only a signboard, which has no real value. To be honest, I do not understand why Ralph invited me to the meeting with Bradley Nichols. I have not won anything more than a paid lunch and a passionless experience. I am sad.

The loss of Fallon torments me like an aggressive nightmare.

"Maggie, will you please come to Pharaohs?" Ed, who is dressed, unusually, in a light blue suit, sneaks up behind me.

"Private Boiler Room shall report immediately!" I say, but choke on my saliva, and the last syllable gets stuck in my throat. "Is it something important?"

"Just come for ten minutes!"

I nod, grab my cup of coffee and follow the boss. Before this, I would also take my notebook, but this time I consider it unnecessary. Anything that Ed could tell me is not worth writing down.

Bright sun shines in Pharaohs, and the Tamm Solutions sales manager closes the blinds with the remote control to diminish the heat. I sit in a chair, drink some coffee and lay the cup on the table. Ed sits down opposite me.

"Maggie, Ralph told me that on the date with Nichols you were very quiet and didn't write down any notes."

For the first time, Ed doesn't bother with a greeting and "how are you?" and immediately reveals the reason for our conversation. *Great. It takes just a couple of minutes, and Mr. Unbearable has reported everything to the boss—again. I said nothing, because I listened. I did not write anything because it seemed unnecessary.* Of course, Ed is interested only in the version told by Ralph, so I cannot afford not to delve into it and keep my thoughts to myself.

"What do you think your strongest qualities are?" Lewis rapidly changes the subject, confusing me. "Can you name them?"

"Love for the profession, desire to learn, loyalty, creativity..." I dispassionately say. Once I identified them with working at *Tamm*, but now? Not really.

Ed takes a sheet of paper that was on the table and runs over the words written there.

"Would you add a sense of responsibility...communication skills...ambition?"

I shrug my shoulders. *I don't know!*

Lewis hands me the sheet of paper, on which a list of characteristics has been written down. In addition, they have been recorded by my teammates about me. *What is going on?*

"I deliberately didn't speak about the Test of Confidence Circle or, as we call it here, the employee's Tamm Gene. We are looking for passion, professionalism, proactivity, creativity, dedication, responsibility, stability, confidence and—

most importantly—a strong team spirit. That is in the gene of all *Tamm* employees. It is important for us that the people we hire in our team are team players, and after the first month of testing each of the team members provides their view of the new employee. Their opinions are written in special way. The good ones are written on the top, the bad ones at the bottom. And at the very bottom there is a place for plus signs, but they are put by the teammate if he or she wants you to be a Tamm employee in the future. I always keep these sheets of paper, as they only for my own evaluation, but I am going to make an exception for you. I would appreciate it if you will not tell your coworkers that you have seen your test page. You can see what is written about you."

I look through the pages, and soon I feel very excited. Carl, Anna and Ralph all see me as a full-fledged coworker! All of them have put pluses at the bottom, and they all have found more positive features than bad ones. They welcome my punctuality, my well-organized work, and my relentless appetite for work. Ralph has even written that my pace of growth is positive. Even Ralph, who told Ed that I am not ready to work with Fallon yet. *What does it all mean?*

"Ed?"

"If you are about to ask about the negative qualities, know that the checklist is completed by each employee in his or her *Tamm* system, so nobody knows what the others have written."

"I am not a team player? How can that be?" My indignation is growing. I know that we have a common goal to achieve, and I work as hard as possible to contribute my share. Why don't they see that?

"On the day when you said that you wanted to leave *Tamm*, I told you that you were finally ready to learn to be a salesperson. You had realized that that you are not powerful. You were free from the old assumptions and ready to create those that would allow you to do your work in an excellent manner. And you're a good student, Maggie, you really are! However, it also seems to me that at the moment, your individual achievements are more important to you."

"I don't know where this misunderstanding has come from!" I object. *It is not true.*

"When I gave Fallon to Anna, what did you think?"

"I thought...that you do not trust me...that you mistakenly think that I would not be able to deal with him! I never thought anything bad about Anna, it was just my deal, and an investment in my KPI!"

"Exactly! *Your* KPI, not *Tamm's* KPI! It was *your* loss, not the transfer of a customer to another, more experienced salesperson! It was *your* failure, not a victory, because in the end you did not continue working with Fallon! What will *you* think of when I've stolen a customer from you? What will *you* think when Ralph supports this theft? What will *you* think when Anna has not defended you and continues the deal with Fallon? What should *you* think, not *Tamm*?"

I lower my head.

"When Ralph invites you to participate in a date, what do you think? And what he must think? Who learns and who teaches? Who grows, and who stays in the same place? How much knowledge does he give to you, and how much knowledge do you give in return?"

I sigh and look at the page. *While I struggled with resentment against them, they have built the same resentment against me. Even with all my growth I have not stepped away from the focus on me, me, me, that Mr. Unbearable reproached me for during my first week of work. Oh God, I have not even said "thank you" to my coworkers yet!*

"And Tom Audrins, Maggie! You knew that the deal was ready to happen even before your date, but it would have been yours. *You* would ring the bell. It would be added to *your* KPI. And Ralph was beside you when you said no, although his instructions and job description confirmed that he was not forced to do it." Ed gets up and put his hands in his pockets. I lay the page on the table. I have nothing to say. "The most stupid thing what you can do now, is to feel guilty about it!"

"I don't understand." *I am guilty in front of the team.*

"It is normal to cling to your accomplishments, to your development. To want everything happen faster! You want to be right there, where Anna or Ralph is, and you think that every obstacle reduces your chance to be equal! Each obstacle makes you sad, angry and offended; but don't forget that we all know what it is like to start something from zero. You will arrive at your destination when you're ready, and not when you catch Ralph in the number of deals you have concluded! You do not have to hurry. You just have to get rid of the assumption that we are enjoying being unfair to you!"

I stopped and thought for a minute. "What should I do?"

"Don't you ever want to be a permanent part of Tamm Solutions? Here, you constantly need to prove yourself. Here, where you do not know how deals will be resolved. Here, where you will have to make cold calls and go to dates. Here, where Ralph is, who will always be better than you, but you will be allowed to challenge him and cast him down from the throne. Here, where 'I can't' is be replaced by 'I can'. Here, where the deal can be transferred to another salesperson with more, highly developed skills. Here, where the only religion is the value map." Lewis paused. "Is that what you want?"

"Yes!" I smile, nodding. "That's what I want!"

"Then, your next task is to trust your team! We are not as evil as you think. Making assumptions does not fit the way we think anymore! Will you be able to do that?"

"Yes, Ed! I'll try!" I grin and bounce on the table. *I have to deal with my emotions and negative assumptions.* The pier emerges in my mind, even more beautiful than before. The road continues to be rough, but I'm not afraid of it. "No, I will not try, I'll do it!"

"Great! Do you want to add anything?"

"No."

"I'll see you tomorrow in the meeting."

I get up and bring the chair to the table.

"Remember Maggie, this does not change your KPI. From now until the end of the test period, you still have to achieve the result we have agreed on."

I collapse, but immediately straighten. *No whining!*

"It's clear!" I grab my cup. At the door, I turn around and I look at the boss. "Ed, I do have something to add."

"Yes?"

"Thank you!" I grin again and leave Pharaohs. Now I understand what had broken in me—an inspiration to go on further. I had no goal and no understanding of why I was doing anything. If, at that time, I had submitted a letter of resignation, it would have been because I thought that I was not useful to Tamm, I was convinced that I did not fit into Tamm Solutions. With Ed's help, that is fixed now. The team wants me to be here, and that is a fantastic inspiration to go on.

I go back to the sales office and throw a glance at my coworkers. I see that Ralph is pointing to the clock. I still have not sent a follow-up to Vincent, and Ralph is signaling that I should do it immediately, otherwise I will get the frog on my desk. I salute and drink the last of my coffee. *Do I have to stop calling Ralph "Mr. Unbearable" after he has given my so much support? Probably not. I'm already got used to it!* I laugh to myself and go to my desk.

"Hey, everybody, what plans do you have for this evening?" I borrow a bit of courage from my stock and make the first step towards liquidating my negative feature, mistrusting the rest of the team.

"I don't have any plans," says Carl, who most of all likes to party.

"What would you say about a team-building event in Old New York?"

Cheers and applause can be heard from around the room, and Ralph begins to laugh. We are all in agreement. Lift up my finger as a sign of victory and smile, looking at Anna. *Everything will be fine.* I'm convinced of it.

Learning to Ask Questions

"You're a savage! Maggie, you will disappear that way!" Ralph mumbles, making sandwich in the kitchen and watching me from the corner of his eye.

"What do you mean?" I look at him. "You don't have to worry about me!"

"I do! If you speak to customers so aggressively, I will have to fire you!"

I put hands on my hips. I don't believe that this is the reason why Mr. Unbearable is in a bad mood. We met with potential customer Sylvia Stennis today, but she did not tell us whether *Polert* will buy our Tamm software. They have had enough time to decide, and such hesitation disturbs the work of our team.

I decided to impose on the woman's feelings. When I told her that four of Polert's five closest competitors use our CRM and in terms of turnover they are much higher position than *Polert*, the naive and meaningless smile disappeared from Stennis's face. *Tamm* teaches us to be humble with customers, but if they do not respect us, I will not be subservient. I have to achieve results rather than polish the pride of some uncertain customer!

"You want to say that she deserved better?"

"No, but that does not change the fact that it was quite unflattering to *Tamm Solutions*! If *Polert* does take our CRM, they will be like a splinter in the behind to you! Believe me, she enjoyed the show more than you did!"

He sneezes, and then Ralph eats his sandwich.

"So, I must be more submissive?"

"I have never said that you must be submissive. Be a professional, focused and humble! That's all! I do not understand why you behaved like that!"

Quite simply, I have reached my third month of work in *Tamm Solutions*, and I realize that I have grown up. My infant diapers and teenage years have been left behind, and now, with a strong backbone, I am standing on the ground. My fire is my professional courage, which has just become a bright flashing light on my pier, and I know that this also matures my genes as a *Tamm* employee. I've learned a lot, including the fact that life is more interesting when you do something, not just try to do. That is my mantra—to do. Not to decide to do something, but to do it. To go and do it. To see and do. Not to sit and wait, but to do. Changes happens only when they make them. There is no other option.

"Maggie, I was looking for you!" Ed enters the kitchen and grabs me by the elbow. "Have you scheduled anything at four o'clock today?"

"No, not that I know about."

"Great! I need you to accompany me to a *Business Angel* investment session."

I'm confused. What is Ed talking about? Ralph makes himself another sandwich and does not say anything.

"I don't think that I will have anything to do there."

"Oh, believe me, you will have a lot to do!" says Ed, smiling.

Is this part of my training? At other times we cannot get the boss to any networking events!

"I realize that I owe you a big debt."

I stare at Lewis, not understanding what he is talking about. *What debt?*

"Continue to finish your most important work, then join me at 3:30 p.m. I will be waiting for you."

Ed nods, and I exchange looks with Ralph. I shrug and return to my desk. With an easy movement, I pull the chair from the desk and laugh. I have got an adjustable chair on castors instead of an ordinary armchair. *Well, Maggie, that's how we grow!*

***

The investment session is taking place in the Business school of a university, giving young entrepreneurs an opportunity to present their business ideas to potential investors and Business Angels. Ed and I are sitting in the guest area meant for spectators, organized in three small rows behind the investors' panel. I get comfortable in the chair. I want to know what these people are going to tell us.

The presentation is opened by a thin young woman with black hair, presenting a makeup application. It by takes a photo of the user's face, offers various day and night make-up options, as well as step-by-step instructions explaining how to apply the makeup yourself. I listen with interest and discover that in a couple of weeks she has collected fifty thousand users, and how additional funding would help to improve the usability of the software product and the introduction of additional features that would be available to paying customers. Investors, who are asked to speak after her presentation, show increased interest in the business model, marketing strategies and competitor research. The girl answers constructively, seeming prepared for almost any issue. I admire her cool mind and her ability to defend her idea. She truly loves her product.

The girl is followed by a young man with a smart bed concept, another guy with a new taxi ordering application, an older engineer who has a bicycle pump innovation, and a young woman with a new type of folding chair. The investors' questions are sometimes cruel and drive the entrepreneur into a dead end of speaking defensively. One entrepreneur successfully manages to get out of the situation, but the other does not. I find it exciting, and only at the beginning of the networking break do I remember that we have not come here for entertainment. That makes me wonder—*why are we here?*

"How do you like these ideas?" Lewis is holding a glass of water.

"Exciting! I did not know that we have such an intelligent youth!"

"You speak as if to represent my generation, Maggie!"

Ed laughs. "Which idea did you like best of all?"

"The make-up application. It was phenomenal!" I turn around to see the thin girl. She stands at the fruit pallet, speaking on the phone. "It was refreshing to hear some other presentations, not only *Tamm's*!"

"What are you going to say about investors and angels?"

Investors and angels? What should I say about them? I was focused on entrepreneurs and I did not pay much attention to the image of others. *It cannot be*, I squint, *that it has a meaning.*

"Investors are obliged to listen and to go into! To understand!" I say in general.

"Anything else?"

I notice how Ed's eyes flicker, and I try to understand how I need to think. What debt he wants to return to me? Why are we here? What is the obligation of investors and angels? I have too many questions, and one event cannot give answers to all of them. *Questions*, I realize. In the test day with Tom Audrins, I made a mistake that led to the situation that Ed did not want to talk to me and left the topic on questions halfway. That is his debt. Now everything is clear!

"Investors are obliged to get more information. And they are doing it by asking questions!" I say.

"Exactly! I want you to go to the investor panel and get three types of their favorite questions."

I wince and hiss. I had to previse that nothing that has to do with Ed Lewis is simple. It this another test?

"And then come back to me."

I smile. If I can deal with *cold* calls and customer complaints, I can also speak with investors and Business Angels on questions.

'Hello," I say to the three victims of examination who stand close to the door and passionately discuss the latest trends in technology products. "Maggie Kent, *Tamm Solutions*!"

"Hello," everyone greets me almost simultaneously. Shake hands with gentlemen and join their conversation, thinking how to turn this conversation effectively and seamlessly to the required direction. *Any ideas?*

"At least for me the most important thing is that the idea is also a business, and particular entrepreneur must understand that. There is a difference whether the idea will be a business or a hobby. I do not know what should happen that I voluntarily invest money in issue that will not give any financial benefit," explains dark haired man who is wearing a black suit with a yellow tie. He has an interesting chin line and strong cheekbones, which together forms quite odd visual image.

"I think that a hobby can turn into a business at a time when person switches on a business thinking," speaks greyish gentleman whose views are the most liberal. He has an extremely kind eyes that makes him more favorite interlocutor than the first one.

"I do not agree! In my practice, there is no such an example," the odd man holds his ground. Oh God, he has a strong negative assumption! "Maggie," he addresses me, "what do you do?"

"I?" I smile. "I am a junior salesperson in *Tamm Solutions*! We are the right arm of business, helping to promote the growth and productivity of companies."

"Really? Interesting! I have not heard of it."

"Maybe it is worthwhile for us to arrange meeting in which I would tell you more details? Perhaps we can help you too!" I say, joking.

"Yes, why not?" the odd one murmurs, and I blink. *I will have a meeting out of nowhere?* He takes a business card from the pocket of his jacket and gives it to me. "Call me next week and we will arrange it."

I thank him and put his business card in my bag with slightly trembling fingers. Unbelievable! *Maggie, the test,* I remind myself.

"I listened the presentation, and your questions were quite direct! Is that how you find out which of them will be businesses and which will be hobbies? "

"Yes!" the odd one says, putting his hands in his pockets. "Today, young people were here, except for the engineer with a pump. In today's youth, I believe, it has already been instilled that they should look where the money is! We are obliged to break or approve their thinking."

"What questions do you ask most often? What helps you to understand?" I asked, thinking that I already approaching the purpose.

"You should remember that questions always have to be big and important!" the liberal reveals. He looks at the odd man.

"For example, I like only one question in one sentence," he continues, "it reinforces the directness! Some of my coworkers unfortunately ask three questions in one sentence, and then wonder that a response is given only to one of them. The last one, or the one the respondent likes best of all! It is not difficult to ask a question and wait for an answer! Then you can continue! Such a philosophy does not make me and the respondent sound like idiots."

"Yes, and also those issues must be complicated and challenging! I'm open for questions, but not those where you have to say yes or no," the odd man says. "You have to understand what you are dealing with! Remember Kaplan, the entrepreneur who spent five minutes explaining the problem that he is struggling with?"

The third gentleman in the dark blue suit nods.

"Five minutes! After his answers it was clear that the entrepreneur had no clarity about his business! If I had not asked a question, I would not have noticed that!"

Simple, non-complex questions. Provocative open questions. What else?

"I agree," the previous gentleman responds in a shrill tone. "I usually ask 'what are you doing; what is your niche; what you have studied?' And so on! I expect a focused response, which I remember from the beginning to the end. In addition, when we know it can also ask about their values."

"Values?" my eyes shine. *Investors also write value maps?*

"Yes, Maggie! We are not fast money seekers. We are working only with entrepreneurs who share the same principles! For example, I always ask how important a reputation is for them, because it is one of our values. And then, how do they ensure that reputation? If the answer satisfies me, we can talk further. Investments are not only the delivery of money, they are formation of a long-term relationship!"

Value questions. I nod - I had not noticed that we used the value card itself as a springboard for further conversation. Thinking about it, Ralph very often uses them to make the client think about his values. *Surprising!* I am glad that the investors have revealed those secrets to me, even without asking.

"And you must not forget that questions should always be logical," the liberal adds, interrupting the flow of my thoughts. *I've already listed three types of questions; are there more?* "Just as you don't ask three questions at once, don't jump over topics! I remember in one interview—I won't say where—at the beginning I was asked questions about my business, then about a job in university where I give lectures, then about my family, and then back to the job in the university again! If you haven't finished all in one question on one subject, don't rush on to another subject! Why do that? It just boggles the mind and does not allow one to think clearly!"

"Asking questions is an art," the gentlemen in the blue suit smiles. "By the way, I have often observed that both investors and entrepreneurs use negative questions in their presentations. And it happens not only in these events, but also in everyday life!"

"Like what?" I am interested. *Logical questions. Positive questions. Five types already*!

"We as a people do not know how to ask positive questions. All the time we look at the other person with suspicion, even if we do not realize it! For example, today the guy offering the taxi application asked, 'wouldn't you want to pay less for a taxi ride?' Why you did he use the word 'wouldn't'?' Why don't we ask, 'would you like to pay less for taxi ride?' It is the same question from two different sides, but only in the second case we would really be inspired to answer 'yes!'"

I remember the story about the girl with the lantern. The admirer also asked questions. That was clearly a part of the test that we did not finish!

"I agree. Negative questions immediately cause negative reactions themselves!" the odd man says. "When I pick up the phone, in 98% of cases the first question is, 'may I disturb you for a minute?' No, you may not! Is what you plan to say so unimportant that it will disturb me? Why do bother calling? Nonsense! Ask permission instead— 'Can I talk to you? Do you have time to talk?' It will make your image more assertive! I also tell my wife that *disturb* is a bad word!" he laughs. The odd man's phone rings. "Just as I expected! Excuse me."

Ask permission. Six types. I remember that I have also asked, 'can I disturb you.' Right away, Ralph told me that it is not the right way to approach potential clients.

"Your day, Maggie, may also be filled with questions!" The liberal is curious.

"Yes, continuously! We have to be able to ask the right questions, because making a contract depends on them." I nod. "Questions help us to understand whether we can help."

Can we help? I ask it in my mind and sigh. I look at Ed, who motions for me to return. *Already?*

"Excuse me! It was nice to talk to you! Have a nice day," I smile. I understand that I cannot disobey the boss.

"How do you feel?" Ed asks.

"Educated! I did not imagine that every question we ask has its own meaning and interpretation—not only *why*, but also *how* and *what* we are asking! It seems that I must learn to speak again!"

"Is there anything else that you noticed?"

"That there are not just three types of questions. There are six...or at least six that investors know about." I smile.

"What did you think when you walked over to them?" The boss looks satisfied. *Apparently, my training is going on according to the plan.*

I take a look at the investors and shake my head.

"Why should I go? What will I say? How will I ask my questions?"

"Maggie, you just showed the progress of a conversation when it is clear what you want to achieve from it!" he says. "There is a reason why I sent you directly to the investors. They are the most skilled professionals at asking questions. And they are so skilled because they clearly know the rules of the game. They know what their goal is! They need to find out who they are going to give the money to, and who not! You also had a goal for this conversation, Maggie, to clarify three types of questions. When you know what you want to achieve, you go and do it! It was not so bad, was it?"

"Not at all. It was even rather interesting. Amusing. Much better than talking about a farmer's market!".

"You'll be able to practice again," Ed reveals. "I want you to go to the entrepreneur of the project that you liked the best and use your newly acquired knowledge about questions to find out all about that project."

The test is not over yet?

"I assume that it will be a makeup application! Let's meet later at the office. You can tell me what you have found out."

I was afraid, but I am no longer afraid. I leave Lewis and go to the dark-haired girl who is enjoying some canapés at the table.

"Hello!" I appear in front of her and smile.

"Hello!" she smiles back at me.

"Maggie Kent, *Tamm Solutions*" I tell her, shaking hands, "I really liked your presentation!"

"Thank you." The girl flushes a bit. Now she looks more vulnerable than in the presentation.

"May I ask you a private question?" I ask permission, following the advice of the odd fellow I spoke with earlier.

The young woman stays silent, watching the expression on my face, and I blink. It happens in a fraction of a second, but it seems as if I see each move of her facial muscles in slow motion. I understand why asking for permission is so important— further conversation depends on it! If the make-up girl says no, the conversation is dead. If she says yes, she will be obliged to answer my question. I can feel the sense of tension of this choice, and it turns me on. I will set up my own catalog of questions that will transform my professionalism, like the sword forged by the most skilled blacksmith.

"Yes," she says.

The game begins!

"How did you get the idea for a makeup application? I know that during the presentation you did not have much time for a detailed story, but I'd love to find out! I'm very interested."

The creator of the application blossoms with a huge smile, and it warms up the entire presentation room. *Compliments and interest create miracles, just like it was with the girl in the red dress.* I also smile more, and we have passed the moment of awkwardness that could have killed our communication a few seconds ago.

Challenges!

This day is not a good day for me. For the first time since the early summer it rains, and it is so dark that I do not even notice that I have to get up. The alarm clock does not ring, either. When I finally climb out of bed and go to the kitchen, I notice that it's already 9:00 a.m. Mumbling, I curse the situation and get ready for work at lightning speed. I am glad that I live only a fifteen-minute walk from the office. I arrive at work shortly before 9:30 a.m. I'm a little wet, but at least I made it to work.

"Oh!" Carl sniggers in excitement. "You get to bring the doughnuts tomorrow!"

Dropping my umbrella beside my desk, I sigh. I take off my coat and join a daily meeting that, to my surprise, still in going on at full force. Usually they do not exceed twenty minutes.

"You get to bring the doughnuts tomorrow," Ralph repeats.

"Yes, I know," mumble. I remember the penalty for being late for the meeting is bringing doughnuts for the whole team. I acknowledge my status as a laggard.

"Let's continue." Ralph, once again, has assumed the role of the head of the meeting during Ed's absence, claps his hands. "Carl, where do you need help?"

"The problem is, where can I get customers?"

"What do you do now?"

"I make cold calls, use the yellow pages in the phone book, relatives, friends and acquaintances." Carl scratches his forehead. "Even Google!"

I grab a notebook from the table—this is an urgent problem for me, too. How nice to arrive at the meeting at the right time to hear this!

"Anna, you have good experience with generating leads." Ralph transfers the baton to our coworker, although I am sure he could name at least ten sources for potential customers.

"Apart from the advertising and PR?" Anna thinks. "Events, such as conferences, seminars and workshops."

Investment sessions, I remark in my mind, remembering the odd investor who unexpectedly agreed to a date. I write down his name on the edge of the sheet and will enter his name in the system after the meeting.

"Internal information," she adds. "There must be a very good circle of existing contacts, but I think this source is the most effective!"

Really? Anna has phenomenal experience with corporate customers in significant IT companies, and she has already attracted many of her contacts, and contacts of contacts, to our CRM. *How can an ordinary salesperson do that?*

"Does putting the Tamm Solutions logo on cars count?" Carl offers. "Or handing out business cards and pens everywhere? Later, can it be written off as marketing expenses?"

"Not bad," Ralph laughs. "By the way, we have never put bumper stickers on cars! Perhaps we should think about that!"

"How can a salesperson find customers? Without having large financial resources?" I sneeze.

"Cheers," Ralph says. "Are there any ideas? It seems to me that if you were to think, you would not be able to get rid of ideas! One of challenges is the diversification of communication!"

What is he talking about?

"There was a time when there was no advertising...when there was no Internet...and people knew that they would be able to find the things they needed by talking to other people. Tell people about yourself, and about our CRM wherever you can. Stories travel a long way! Use your partners and existing customers! Go to associations and collect information. Visit unions, tourist centers and chambers of commerce, where brochures and contacts are available. Be creative, do not focus on just one medium. It will be good for both the salesperson and the buyer."

"Meet a girl for dinner and tell her about Tamm!" Carl suggests. "If she is not the love of your life, maybe she will become a customer!"

"That's creative enough. Why do you tell me that you have problems finding customers?" Ralph motions to a coworker. "Instead of staring blankly out of the window, begin a conversation on the public bus! Find out who the people are around you! I meet Ed that way. He was sitting next to me on the subway to Brooklyn. Without that conversation, I might never have come to work in Tamm Solutions."

Leads are everywhere! I carefully write down the sources they have named so I won't forget any of them. I also look at the phone directory, still standing on the shelf and waiting for the next victim. I have a plan to use it shamelessly for my needs. Now I have the right to do so!

"Just do not forget to qualify your leads," Ralph admonishes. "You know that not all of them will become our customers."

"That's easy!" Anna exclaims. "We need to know whether they need us, and we need to find the decision-makers. Then you can really start to talk!"

"What about other aspects? Where they are located, what is the industry and the size of their team?" Carl asks.

"Of course, those are also important! And check if they have money!" Mr. Unbearable smiles ironically. "Did we answer your question?"

Carl nods.

"Maggie, what is your news?" Ralph focuses on me.

"Without doughnuts?"

"Without doughnuts!"

I tell them about yesterday's achievements, at the same time thinking of about strategies to find new customers. It is particularly important right now—this is the last month of my probation period with the company.

***

"Very good!" Fallon studies an agreement about the status of his adviser, prepared by Tamm. We offer something like that for the first contract. Both parties involved want the rules to be clear and very carefully developed. Reputations, technical skills, promises and a hundred thousand dollars are in the game. There has been so much tension, you would think the future of the country depended on this contract. "I will give it to our lawyer and the head of the IT department to make sure that we all understand it the same way!"

"Of course," Anna quietly replies. We are meeting in Pharaohs, where the familiar walls help to mask our excitement.

I sit next to Anna and watch, curious about what will happen. Fallon occasionally smiles at me as if to say, "don't worry," but the very next moment he takes the opportunity to ask a tricky question.

"Will I, as the advisor, have access to a completely different control panel than the others?"

In fact, I had not expected that my initiative would lead to such landslide of problems. Originally, I had outlined an initiative that included testing capabilities and priority service; now we are discussing advantages such as access to programming codes for certain functions, and regular meetings with *Tamm's* programmers, who will be required to implement Fallon's wishes.

So far, Anna has diplomatically stated that *Tamm* is a professional and independent company that is not under the umbrella of Metals LLC and does not have to disclose its trade secrets to Metals LLC, but it certainly does not lessen the Smart Client's attempts to impose his own rules. Well, now I see the risks that Ed warned me about when this customer was transferred to Anna, and I am pleased that it has happened this way. Fallon continuously snoops and checks our boundaries, and I certainly would not be able to handle him on my own.

"The control panel is different for each customer because every company has its own needs, and specific functions help them to do their work. This is also true for you, Mr. Fallon; it will be adapted to give you exactly what you need." Anna is cold and dispassionate, despite the psychological pressure. She is standing on the front line of a battle. She has the firmness needed to work with major customers. If Ralph has humility, then Anna has humility and firmness. "If the customer sees that they can order you about, the deal will be lost," were her words.

Fallon looks confident and nods, agreeing to Anna's remarks, and that calms me down. We agree to prepare answers to some additional questions, and the date is over. The head of Metals LLC leaves Tamm Solutions' office pretty quickly, and we have now been loaded with a new stack of tasks.

"Large customers are unpredictable, Maggie," Anna says on the way to the kitchen. "Very often they make you to feel like a house without a foundation. When that happens, just sit them out because they are trying to check how strong you are."

"What major problems have you had with big customers?"

"I could write a book about that!" Anna fills her cup with coffee. "There are a lot of risks! Some of them do not pay invoices - all the time they are good, when they have to make the payment, cannot find them. Trying to use unethical practices—it seems that Fallon constantly tries to add new items to the contract when we have already agreed on what is included. Some customers show personal, sexual interest. Many female salespeople have to deal with that!"

"Sexual interest?"

"Yes, unfortunately." Anna drinks a sip of coffee. "A female salesperson, above all, is a woman. Every male customer initially evaluates you as a woman when you walk into the room! Then their interest arises, and it greatly affects the stability of the deal! Believe me, it will happen at least once in your career too!"

I sit there in horror, but Anna ignores it. *She doesn't care about it. Why?*

"If it happens, how do you deal with it?"

"You must remain professional! You have to say no to the offers to for dinner and say no to flowers and other gifts! The trick is, you must refuse so that it does not offend the customer! Say no in a way that does not offend his ego!"

"That's hard to do!"

"Yes, it is, but ethical principles have to come first if want to keep your job!"

I sigh, hoping that Anna's prediction will never come true.

"In fact, the main thing you have to remember about large deals is to stay alert!"

"That's interesting. Why is it so important to stay alert?"

"When we get a large customer, at first, we have a tendency to reduce the speed, because we've done our job and we feel that everything is going great. It is deceptive! If you not continue to make deals, there will be the hole the next month. Do not allow that to happen! I'm speaking from personal experience."

"Thank you!" I smile. "I will remember that!"

"Second, it's one thing is to conclude a deal, but quite another to deliver it! Large customers will be sharp-eyed and look for deficiencies. Your obligation is to eliminate those deficiencies in a timely manner and deliver the transaction. Fallon is an entrepreneur who cares about his own interests. Only a fully completed transaction will bring the money into our account!"

I nod. I'm looking forward to finally getting past the contract signing period and being able to start work as an advocate for Fallon. In fact, Fallon will set a precedent for further development of the advisor program, and I believe that by working together with Anna it will be successful.

***

It is still raining. I sit in the CSC and watch the raindrops hitting the windowsill.

Raindrops have no chance in front of fate; they are at the mercy of the wind. If raindrops could think, would they would choose to fall against the windowsill? How much would they worry about their world if they were alive? What would my fire do, if understood that it cannot resist the raindrops?

It becomes darker, and I am sleepy. The gentle sound of the rain is an outstanding lullaby.

Maggie, concentrate! Blinking my eyes, I drink some coffee. *I have to get back to work!* I am filling in reports in Tamm's CRM system. I open the contact file where I have stored the phone numbers of the translation agencies that I just found in *Google*. Those contacts are extremely *cold*, but I can try them anyway.

Two messages simultaneously appear in my e-mail, and I bend closer to the screen of computer, as if trying to read the messages before they've been opened. One is from Raymond Vincent, and the other is from Sylvia Stennis. *Interesting!*

I open the message from Mr. Customer first. He has kindly replied a week after my letter to him. I wonder why any news arrives from him at all, considering our relationship and the frequency of our correspondence.

Good afternoon,

I thought that you had forgotten about us. As we already agreed in the meeting, we will not take Tamm Solutions.

Have a nice day,

Raymond Vincent

I bang my fist on the table. *What is with this man?* Mumbling in anger I stand up. *When did we agree? When he ignored me? Or when he told me that I know where the exit is and can find my own way out? Idiot!* After a minute, the rain calms me, and I lean against the wall. *I cannot control the thoughts of others*, I point out to myself. *You should be happy that Mr. Customer does not need Tamm's CRM. Sit down and write a reply.*

Good afternoon,

Thanks for the information.

Have a nice day,

Maggie Kent

I hope that Sylvia has written something better.

Hello,

I have submitted the topic of Tamm's CRM system for tomorrow's Board meeting. Do you have time tomorrow to come and tell the members of Board the same information that you told me? Then we will be able to take a decision immediately.

Yours,

Sylvia Stenne

Head of Polert Development Department

I hit my head against the table. We have discussed this several times already. They already know *everything*. I press the reply button and type.

Hello Sylvia,

Yes, of course, I will come to the Board meeting. Do I remember correctly that it begins at 9:00 a.m.? It is possible that I will bring a few of my associates with me.

See you tomorrow,

Maggie Kent

I send the email and shrug, then book the date in Tamm's calendar system and invite Ralph to participate in it. We will do almost anything for the deal, right? For a moment, I turn the chair, and look at the poster on the wall. *The receiver is not the enemy.* I straighten my back. *Maggie, where did you stop? Let's not waste time!* I pick up the phone and start my session, trying to collect more contacts. I dial the number of the first translation office.

"Hello?" a man's voice responds.

Let's go!

***

The rain continues during the evening, but it does not prevent me from meeting a classmate who I have not seen for two years. We meet in a wine bar in Chelsea and sip an excellent Chardonnay at a small table.

"I never thought that would go to into programming." Lisa, a true hipster with many tiny braids, laughs. "You know how I loved algebra! Incredible!"

Lisa loves to be the center of attention, and that is one of reasons why it was not easy to get along with her during our school years. We got along very well, mainly because I was not interested in extra attention; mom taught me that a person's works say much more about them than a fur coat shop bought in an expensive shop.

"What are you doing?" Lisa asks, sipping the wine. "I remember that wanted to be a salesperson!"

"Yes, I have succeeded!" I wink. Unlike my mother and Erica, Lisa has never thought my dream career was unimportant, probably because for quite a long time we were excited about the teachings of Tony Robbins. "I am a salesperson in one of the nicest technology enterprises—Tamm Solutions!"

"Tamm Solutions?" Lisa raises her eyebrows. "I know of them! You are a big player! Super, Maggie!"

"Yes, now we try to land a large customer." I blush, enjoying my friend's support. "It's hard, but soon it will be done! We could be pioneers, because as far as I know, no one else in New York is doing this."

"A large customer?" Lisa becomes noticeably curious. She puts her glass on the table and leans closer to me. "Are you talking about Oliver Fallon?"

Suddenly, I become cautious. *How would Lisa know about Tamm Solutions and Oliver Fallon? What has happened?* Cold shudders run through my body. *If she works for a software development company, does this mean that Fallon is still looking for alternatives? No, it can't be! Is this the reason why the contract has not been signed yet?*

"What can you tell me?" My pulse speeds up to double time. I hope that our friendship is worth enough to disclose the goings-on of another company. *Internal information.* Anna mentioned it as a good source for leads, but my source can immediately offer up an Advisor program that has not been launched yet.

"Nothing much, Maggie. Just the fact that one of the *Metals LLC* board members is really pushing the topic that the company needs a different CRM software because Tamm Solutions is disproportionately expensive! Although Fallon will make the final decision, he is investigating whether he can find something cheaper. I don't know anything about the amounts involved, though."

I turn pale. *Fallon has not said anything. Now I begin to understand why he is pushing our limits—he can always say no! This is awful!*

"You didn't hear it from me!" Lisa exhales. "I'm only telling you that because you're my friend. In my opinion, Fallon is an idiot. At the same time the contract is being negotiated, he is investigating other opportunities!"

"Don't worry, no one will find out from me! Do you know whose CRM he wants?"

"I'm not involved in this project, so I will not be able to find out."

Maintain alertness, Anna said. Alert signals are going off throughout my body. They continuously stab into my heart, my knees, my brain. *Drink some more wine, it will help me to think. Maggie, think!* For a moment, I look at Lisa and wonder if I can trust her. Sigh—*of course, I can trust her.*

"What do you think? How much time we have?" *I cannot believe that I'm asking that.* Even today, Fallon said that his lawyers will review the contract and he will sign it. *Does he have such little respect for us that he would lie to us to fool us?* My sense of anger and fear increases.

Lisa lifts up her shoulders, and I see that I am at a dead end. *What can do I with this information?* If Fallon wanted to pull the rug out from underneath my feet, he has succeeded.

Saving the Deal

Finally, Polert says yes! The Board
meeting runs smoothly, and at the end we
shake hands and agree when the contract
will be signed. I am particularly proud that
I have carried the entire load on my own
shoulders. Both Ralph and Ed agreed that
it is finally time for me to learn to face
customers alone. Now I am convinced that
like the best Tamm professionals, I have
ability to conclude the deal in the
opponent's arena. It turns out that the
assertiveness I practiced yesterday has
brought me the desired result.

The sales bell is in my hands again, and I
am ringing it as loudly as possible. Its
sound is clear, and I swear that each time
it sings a different song. I close my eyes
and breathe in the smell of victory. I see
my coworkers applauding me, but I do not
hear them. They stay at their desks and do
not come over to me. My heart hears and
feels only the song of the bell. It belongs to
me.

True, the more it rings, the spookier it
becomes. The sound is no longer clear. It is
a stiff and dull, and it seems to me that
someone has taken away the joy. *What is
going on?*

I close and open my eyes, and I see the
void. *How can Fallon can be so heartless?*

I try to smile and put the bell back on the shelf.

"Great!" The voice I hear sounds like it is in a barrel, and I barely recognize that it is Ralph. "Carl, I hope you follow Maggie's example, otherwise you will never get rid of the frog!"

Squinting, I see the green frog symbolizing that work has not been done. It has been standing on Carl's desk for several days. For me, Fallon also stays in the row of unfulfilled successes.

"Maggie, I'm waiting for the next one," Ed says, standing behind me. I open my mouth to reveal that Fallon is a villain, but a weight presses on my lungs and the words evaporate before they can come out of my mouth.

I nod and go to the table. I have to make up my mind not to cry when I tell my coworkers about that. I do not want Ralph, Ed, and Anna to think that I am falling apart, that I do not know how to behave properly. I still have to prove that I can take good decisions in high stress situations.

I open the calendar and fill in the information about the Polert deal in the system and send the follow-up to Stennis, so that we can proceed immediately. In addition, I have four dates during the next few days, hoping that another positive result will complete the KPI for my test period.

This time my smile is warmer. *It is not as bad as thought. Can I control the choices Fallon makes? No! Can I control his actions? No! Can I say when and how he needs to act? No! Then it makes no sense to worry! It's true that we would not recover the resources we've spent, but no one would say that we haven't done enough to conclude this deal.*

Wait Maggie! I mentally slap myself. *Fallon has not disappeared. He is still here! He is like a pale shadow, but it's not over yet! I will not cry. And I will not allow negative thoughts to steal the joy of a successful deal with Stennis. Nope!* Leaning back in chair, I turn to the window. It is still raining, and I look for a little more strength inside myself that will help me to find a solution to the challenge of the Smart Client. I do not believe that there is no solution. There has to be a way!

***

'Team Ed" enters the sales office in the afternoon, holding a large curled paper under his arm. He looks worried, and that is not usually the case with him. We watch how he demonstratively sticks the sheet with names of salespeople written on it to the nearby wall behind the sofa. "So, team! I have fantastic news!"

"Fantastic news" usually means a change in the situation and maintaining our competitive spirit. Ed always makes sure that Tamm's salespeople will not rest on their laurels in the workplace.

"Let's start from the beginning! Some of you know that every August *Tamm* has a great team-building event that bring together all our American offices. Yesterday I called Washington. The event will be in three weeks!"

My co-workers clap their hands and begin to discuss what entertainment can be expected at the events.

"More information will be available later but be prepared for both entertainment and hard work. We have planned the biggest boiler room in Tamm's history!"

My colleagues become a quieter, but this does not seem to diminish their enthusiasm. I am eager to get acquainted with the salespeople in the other offices.

"Team, that is not all! Washington has decided that our New York office can do more than it is doing at the moment, so that is why this sheet had been created." He gets closer to the sheet. "This month, I expect forty deals from you instead of the current twenty!" The boss writes *Deals 40* on the top of the sheet. "Each of you should work harder this month and deliver at least ten deals to *Tamm*."

My hands sweat. *This is nonsense. It doesn't apply to me, does it? I have made one deal in two months, and I have to get nine deals in the third month? I can't sign on to such a drastic change in expectations!*

"This means that our KPI changes?" Ralph smiles.

"No, you still have twenty," Lewis smiles back. "This," he points to the number at the top of the sheet, "is the minimum!"

Well, of course, it's nothing for Mr. Unbearable!

"But yes, the KPI changes! For everyone." His gaze settles on me.

Ok, let it be. I am indignant. *My test period has already been a huge challenge, so why shouldn't I get buried by their expectations at the end of it?*

"Why do you look like that?" Ed comes to us. "You live in an environment where you have to be in the best form all the time! *Tamm* is not a comfort zone," he straightens up, his finger pointing to the honorary poster, "because then nothing would grow! Don't whimper! If I know that you couldn't do it, you wouldn't be here! To help you, I am looking forward to seeing each of you on Friday for one-to-one sessions to discuss how you can achieve our new goal! I will send your session times later. So, let's get to work!" he points. "Oh, please write the names of companies opposite your name on the sheet! We will maintain the spirit of competition, as it is the motivation for others to act! The best salesperson of the month will have a special prize!"

Eyes of Ralph and Carl blink - they have accepted the challenge. What do I have to do? I do not want to complain that I cannot get it. *Then do not complain,* pointing to myself, *only take twice as much effort to make everything succeed.* If all potential dates say yes, then I will complete the old KPI. If I get five more, then I would also fill the new KPI. Is it possible at all?

***

"How trustworthy is this information?" Ed is frighteningly serious.

"Very!" I have taken the initiative and invited Ed Lewis, Anna and Ralph to Vizier to tell them about the danger related to the Smart Customer's deal. "My source says that Fallon is even considering creating his own CRM!"

"Doesn't he understand the value of our system?" Ralph asks. "I have the impression that he likes to bargain.

Customers who behave so unreliably make me furious!"

Bargain? How can we find a compromise with Oliver Fallon?

"Let's do a follow-up!" Anna suggests. "Once again, we'll find where we stand with him, and request an answer. Today! The longer we will hesitate, the more power we will give him."

"I agree! Let's work on that," Ralph says. "It will be more honorable if we are the ones to say "no."

"What are our scenarios?" Ed puts his hands in his pockets. "When we talk to him, it is important to be prepared for various outcomes."

"I do not think that any other outcomes are available now, Ed! He has a contract, an offer and the time - that is enough to decide!"

"Ralph," the boss calls us to order. "What is selling?" Ed pauses and looks at each of us. "It is the ability to convince the other party that they need what you are offering them! It is also ability to make concessions. Once you have determined what can happen, you will not be surprised when it does. This is known as 'the realization of alternatives.'"

There is silence in Vizier. I tap my fingers on my leg to use my extra energy.

"We can react to Fallon in time. Tell me, what is the best thing that could happen?"

"He will take the whole package, the amount we have agreed on will remain unchanged, and the terms will be as they are now," I say, trying to fit into the conversation.

"That is the ideal option," Ed agrees.

Do you realize, Maggie, that by playing these games Fallon can betray Tamm? He could also decide to go through with the deal and become the first deal concluded on my list of KPIs.

"Then you need to know your strongest points and the customer's weakest points in order to make those scenarios effective!" Ralph says.

"Exactly!" the boss sits down.

What are my strong points? And what are Fallon's weak points? The fact that I know about his hypocritical performances? Or is that my weakest point and the strongest one for him, as I could lose Fallon after all? Oh God, why everything is so complicated?

"We also can bargain, Ralph, according to your comment!" Lewis continues. "We need to know on what basis we can refuse Fallon...and what we will definitely not refuse!"

"Ed, that has already been discussed in the contract negotiations," Anna comments. "He wants access to the system code, and that will not happen! He wants access to future technical solutions, and that will not happen either! This is the core of Tamm's business. If we give the code for our software to anyone, we will soon be out of business! Ed, Fallon wants power, and we cannot let him have it the way he wants it! The deal needs to be exactly what it is in the contract, without any changes! This time, I agree with Ralph—go all in! If not, then everything will be over!"

Everything? How do we go "all in"? A defense mechanism suddenly switches on in me. *Are we going to give up so quickly, if the answer from Fallon is no? Where is the challenge in giving up? Fallon is my deal—I found him! It sounds conceited, but it is the truth! I'm willing to bargain if necessary!*

"Ok, I will review the contract again, and I'll see if we can do something." Ed says. "Maggie, please, arrange a meeting with Oliver, preferably tomorrow—say that we need to discuss the implementation details and the initial steps of his involvement in testing some *Tamm* functions that have not been released yet. Say anything to get him to agree to the conversation!"

Nodding, I agree. It is an action plan. *This is the solution.* I sigh, relieved. *We will keep on fighting!*

"Ralph, Anna, I understand you, but let's work on it a little bit more. Let's go back to the value map and explain it again. I want you to recognize that we always take risks when we're talking, but as the leaders we must be able to do it!"

I'm not a leader, but I am inspired by Ed's words. He is a fighter, and I will follow him till the end.

Anna and Mr. Unbearable are silent. This time, there is no power in their arguments. And they do agree, although they indicate that such an evil customer is not worthy of getting our CRM. They are right, but we have come too far to stop at this point.

***

Fallon is not responding. Not to phone calls, not to e-mails. His secretary says he has a meeting, and l go on just out of curiosity, I ask whether it will go on all day. We have not yet signed a contract to work together, but each of us already defends our own truth. I want to do something reckless, like visiting Fallon at his office to see how available he actually is. It would be aggressive, and contrary to the Tamm rule of humility, but it would be the only way to visit the lion in his den. I give up on this idea and go on to other work.

I am glad that the Smart Customer's attitude gives me extra incentive to make cold calls. Within three hours I have arranged three more dates for the next week, and now Ed's torture sheet, hanging on the wall, does not seem as problematic. *Maybe cold calls are my vocation*, I laugh to myself, entering the information about the dates in the CRM system. I look also at the profile case. It has been filled with so much valuable knowledge during the last two months that soon there will not be enough space to add any more information. Just yesterday, inspired by pressure surrounding the Fallon deal, I added a new sticky note in order not to forget what a good salesperson is.

***

I am lost in my thoughts. I hope that I meet at least the minimum KPI that will allow me to stay here after the test period.

"Maggie?" Ed comes to me. "What news do you have about Fallon?"

"He was still in a meeting half an hour ago."

"Call again," he tells me, firmly. "Now! And switch on the speaker."

I pick up the phone and call. I am convinced that this number soon will be added to Metals LLC's blacklist. Beep! I put the receiver on the table and look at Lewis—he has a serious expression. Third beep. *Interesting, what is he thinking about now?* Fifth beep.

"Hello!" a woman's is on the other end of the receiver. I am a little embarrassed because it's Oliver Fallon's phone number, but then I recognize that it's his secretary.

"Hey, Justine!"

"Hello!"

"Maggie from Tamm Solutions here!"

"Hello," she says again. I suspect that she recognized the phone number before she answered the call.

"Sorry that I seem to be chasing you today! Is Mr. Fallon available? We should make an appointment to talk about the final details for Tamm Solutions' implementation process. It is important to have this meeting as soon as possible!"

"I understand. Unfortunately, Mr. Fallon is still in a meeting. May I ask him to call you back?"

"Approximately when he would be available today?"

"It is hard to say."

"Maybe you can schedule an appointment for tomorrow? As I said, it is quite important for us in order to proceed in the most successful way."

"Unfortunately, it will not be possible within the next two weeks," secretary swallows her saliva. "Mr. Fallon is going on vacation tomorrow!"

Damn it, is this a joke? Do we need another sign to comprehend finally that the battle is lost? I am watching Ed who gestures that I should hang up.

"I understand! Then please tell him to call me back so that we can agree on the time after his vacation."

"Definitely, Maggie. Bye!" I hear a smile in the secretary's voice, and she hangs up.

I look at the phone and cannot understand my emotions. *This is a complete defeat.* My heart feels heavy. It delights and saddens me.

"He will not really take a vacation, right?" I am fascinated by Fallon's potential cowardice. He, as an experienced entrepreneur, should have known that in business honesty is a primary requirement.

"Do you think that *Tamm* fits Fallon?" Ed suddenly asks. He reviews my profile case and then looks at me, and there is something I don't understand in his gaze.

"Yes! One hundred percent! We're perfect for him."

"Then let's go!"

"Where are we going?" I blink.

"To Metals LLC! Let's go, Maggie," he urges. "We shall try Ralph's technique. Let's go till the end!"

I grab my bag and stand up.

"We will do what others don't," Ed says, "let's go till the end to get the customer back!"

Ok, good, I nod. *But we should not do it,* my caution and disbelief speaks within me. *It is aggressive. You had the same idea,* I say. *Terrible. Is this it really happening?*

Ed grabs the keys for the company car, and off we go. Only the two of us. *Like Batman and Robin, we will defend the honor of Tamm Solutions. We will win, or we will learn.* An adrenaline bomb explodes inside me, and now I would be willing to follow Ed Lewis anywhere, even to the president. *This deal will happen. Will not happen. Will happen. Will not happen. It will!*

***

The offices of *Metals LLC* are located near the cruise passenger terminal, and they can see ships entering the port from their windows. That does not diminish the panic that has caused my surging adrenaline. All the way there I sit in the car and tremble, even when Ed starts a conversation. I could not understand a word that he said. Even now, when we are sitting in the lobby, my heart beats crazily. *This is not a good idea. We will lower ourselves and tell him how much we correspond to their value map, but we will not be able to persuade him. I never want to see Fallon again.* For all I care, he can make millions of CRMs, but even his best attempts will never reach the elegance of Tamm Solutions' software.

"Hello," a beautiful brunette in a green pant suit welcomes us. She is one of Fallon's secretaries—I know her voice. "Today Mr. Fallon is busy!"

"Hello," Ed takes over the conversation, "we appreciate his time! We only need five minutes!"

I hope I will not need to talk. I would not be able to. I am thankful that I will be able to watch Ed in action, but I will not talk.

"Maggie?" The boss grips me.

"What?"

"Come on!"

Yes! It seems that Ed has won a seat at Fallon's round table of Fallon if, of course, he has one. I will fall. The pier will fall with me. Sad! Who am I trying to fool? I'm not even close to a good salesperson yet.

We are entering the meeting room. There is no round table, but everything is yellow, both walls and furniture. *Nasty! What do I have to do? Where is my ability to concentrate? Ability to listen? Ability to be a professional?* It seems that Fallon will cut our tongues out and give them to the jesters of his court, or at least to those who will make his special CRM.

"Maggie!" Ed grip me by shoulders. "What's happened to you?"

"I am afraid."

"Afraid of what?"

"The outcome!"

"Why?"

"I don't know!" I mutter, and the strange thing is that I really do not know. I do not want anyone to trample over me. Self-esteem prefers that I remain aloof, not stand in the center of a disaster.

"I can suggest only one thing. Have fun!"

What? Surprised, I look up at him.

"What happens when we are afraid?" the boss asks me.

"Our protective mechanisms turn on."

"And when do they turn on?"

"When we are fighting to stay in our comfort zone!

"Do not forget that during a date!" Lewis smiles, and it takes away most of my fear. "Isn't that the reason why we put our hand on the comfort zone poster every morning, to test ourselves and remember to think outside the box?"

I am little ashamed, because I still have not touched it. *I was afraid, but I am no longer afraid*, I say to myself. Then I count to ten and realize that my panic has gradually faded into the background. Smart Customer, together with an older gentleman, joins us. I find the nicest smile in my arsenal and shake hands with both of them. *This is not so bad. It does not seem that Oliver will treat us badly.*

"Sorry that you had to wait," Fallon says after we have greeted each other and been introduced to the older man. It turns out that he is Ernest Dauga, the Director of Development at Metals LLC, and I wonder whether he is the one who is trying to persuade Fallon to create their own CRM system.

"Today it is very busy and a little tense around here. Tomorrow I go on vacation, and I wanted to settle the priority issues before leaving."

I inhale slowly. *He really is going on vacation? It seems pretty short-sighted of him not to let us know about that in a timely manner!*

"I do not understand your haste. I was going to call you to transfer this issue to a later date. It would also allow our lawyers to re-examine the merits of the contract," he continues.

'Thank you. I understand." Ed organizes his jacket. "The reason why we are here is directly related to your vacation, Mr. Fallon. We want to understand whether we have correctly recorded your needs!"

"I could have told you that on the phone!" Fallon twists in the chair.

I was afraid, but I am no longer afraid. I try to analyze what Fallon's position is, and what impact Dauga has on Fallon.

"Yes, it was our choice," Ed smiles. "As we are here, we would love to hear your thoughts on the current offer! Can we improve anything? If there are any questions, I think that Maggie will be able to answer them."

Me? No! I will not talk! My tight tone of voice would certainly indicate that I feel offended—and frightened.

"As far as I know, there are no problems." Fallon shakes his head. He is hiding.

I am glad that there is a pitcher of water and some glasses on the table. I pour myself a glass and drink a sip, and now I feel a little better.

"I will reveal that we are still discussing the price," Dauga says. His voice is hollow, and it does not suit his facial features. "For so much money we could make our own CRM, which will do what we want!"

Yes, bingo! Dauga stands between Tamm and Oliver Fallon. Listen, Maggie!

"Moreover, the fact that our data will be stored on your servers, rather than ours, is absurd! We have faith in our servers but not so much in yours. It's nothing personal – our data safety standards do not allow us to store our sensitive information with third parties!"

Surprised, I realized that Dauga is the real source of the objections! No wonder he does not understand anything—Fallon does not know how to transfer the value to his Board, and that is what is blocking the deal. My panic is gone, and I am willing to unmask Dauga's objections. *Why doesn't Ed say anything?*

"We also want to work with a more experienced team." Ernest Dauga finishes and leans back in his chair.

"Yes, you must know that we are evaluating the alternatives as well!" Fallon adds.

Silently, I take a breath.

"That is clear." Ed leans forward and looks at Dauga, eye to eye. "When you say that you are thinking about developing your own CRM software, how do you see it? How have you imagined your system?"

"We see it as one we can control," Dauga states. "You know how it is, Mr. Lewis. Each new investment has to be evaluated seven times. I can tell you that we already know we can have our own CRM, that will meet our needs, and at a lower cost!"

"Of course, Mr. Dauga, it is true—investments need to be measured." *Ed looks like the stone wall that Dauga wants to destroy. Let's see if he will succeed.* "Investment needs to be rethought for the long-term. I hope that your calculation for the development costs includes the maintenance of system that needs to be carried out whenever a threat appears in it, and the costs of the updates, because almost every day new integrations and new functions to assist your work will appear, and of course there is the cost of training your staff how to use the system most effectively, and 24 hour support if anything we just mentioned does not work properly! And I am not speaking about only the human resources needed to operate all that!"

Dauga grows pale.

"This is part of the value we provide to our customers." my boss says. "In addition, for you, as the adviser, these benefits are provided on a priority basis! My question is, do you need a CRM that works in your favor independently from you or in continuous dependence?"

Here it comes. I bite my cheek in order not to smile. *Our CRM's costs are insignificant when compared to the cost of developing and maintaining a CRM by a single company.* Metals LLC will recover the one hundred thousand dollars in a ridiculously short time. Dauga bends forward and regroups. *Apparently, he is not accustomed to defending his position.*

"It's your choice, of course!" Ed returns the power of decision-making to Dauga. "I also want to clarify the issue regarding data security," and quickly takes back this power. *The second round starts now.* I look at Fallon, who has no intention of getting involved. *Could he deliberately have put Dauga in the cross-fire to get extra votes in favor of Tamm? Maybe he is not a bad guy in this story after all?* "If I understand correctly, you have your own servers?" my boss asks.

Dauga nods.

"And you don't want to entrust your data to the cloud?"

Dauga nods again. *Ask simple questions*, I remember.

"I can assure you that for Tamm Solutions, data security is our highest priority! All security settings are regularly inspected and updated. This also is an additional investment you should not worry about, because we will do it for you."

"I do not trust the cloud." *Dauga does not give an inch.*

"Can I ask what e-mail service provider you use? Both for Metals LLC, and for private needs, perhaps?"

"Google! Gmail!"

"And do you also use any storage site, such as DropBox?"

"Yes."

"Then you are already using the cloud. Often people see the cloud as a threat, however, experience has shown that it is one of the highest achievements of modern technology, used by almost all companies in the world, including Google and Metals LLC! And we will also take care of this security aspect so that you can fully indulge in the growth of your company and increased sales figures. The control remains in your hands, we just provide the technical solutions."

Ernest Dauga is reassured, I see it in his eyes. *He is ready to buy our CRM software solution*. He looks at Fallon, nods slightly, and I am willing to bet that there is no longer any question about which CRM Metals LLC will choose.

"Finally, I would like to mention the competency of Tamm Solutions' team!" Ed continues, and without mentioning Dauga's turning in favor of him. *He is an excellent salesperson and listener—he remembers all the arguments even without writing them down.* I am caught up! "We do our work with the highest professional and ethical principles, and I can assure that your status as the advisor has been evaluated. I'm not talking only about our salespeople, but also our project managers and programmers. Your opinion is important to us. It will allow us to make the product even better, and to help you more effectively!"

"Can you guarantee that you will be able to deliver what is written in the contract?" Fallon finally engages in the discussion. First, he looks at Lewis, and then he focuses on me.

My panic returns. *I will not talk. I do not know how to talk! I was afraid, but no longer afraid. Oh God - I cannot take part with my amateur portrayal after such a game as Ed has played!*

"Yes!" The words stick in my throat and does not sound as convincing as I would like. "Yes," I try again, and this time it sounds better. "You'll be the advisor, and you will be entitled to have everything that is written in the contract!"

Fallon and Dauga both nods. *Great, we're back in the game!*

"Let's continue this when I return from my vacation." The Smart Customer gets up.

"Unfortunately, we don't have enough time!" Lewis also stands up, and I follow his example. What does he mean, not enough time? "The advisor program is only available for a limited time, and we have to know the answer. This is another reason why we're here!"

Fallon's face looks sour. *He no longer has the power to decide when this deal will be concluded. Is Ed aggressively humble, or is something like that possible at all? It's fantastic, but risky.*

"What is your offer?" the Smart Customer asks.

Will there be more bargaining? I was afraid, but I am no longer afraid. I step away a little further, thus leaving space for the personalities of both men to push against each other. *Maggie, you won't often experience anything like this!*

"The offer has not changed. Metals LLC has the status of adviser and that means, first, the growth of company development and productivity and, second, it allows you to create your perfect CRM system in collaboration with *Tamm Solutions*!" Ed is diplomatic. "Do we have a deal?" he stretches out his hand, completely heating up the atmosphere in the room.

Lewis has an effect because he owns what Fallon and now Dauga want. The Smart Customer is also aware that whatever happens in this room will be final. It will be a victory or a lesson, but we will be winners in either case. I was afraid, but I am no longer afraid, I remind myself, my blood bubbling like a geyser from the excitement. What will Fallon do? He looks at Ed's hand, and I do not understand why he hesitates if he is on our side anyway. Inside myself, where the customers cannot hear it, I take a deep breath and sigh. *Do we still have more bargaining to do?*

The Importance of a Handshake

The date is over, and I'm looking out through the car window. We are driving back to Tamm Solutions, and my nervous anxiety has overtaken me. The experience at Metals LLC has left me speechless, and I cannot stop thinking how close to the abyss we came, searching for the way out of a hopeless situation with Oliver Fallon. I needed so much courage to conquer my fear! I needed so much courage to convince them that we were telling the truth! I needed so much courage to finally shake their hands and conclude the deal.

"Sometimes you have to do things aggressively and creatively to sustain a deal," Ed says.

"Were you scared?"

"All of us are afraid, Maggie! All salespeople. Me too!"

"You didn't answer my question!"

"I did not, you're right." Lewis thinks. "I was scared at the moment when we decided to go. Then the fear really had no place. You do what you have to do!"

"It felt like I was going to die!"

"It seemed so, for a moment! Maggie never be afraid of any decision you make. Now do you understand now why I gave Fallon to Anna?"

"Yes," I say and nod. *I realized that much earlier.*

"What can you say about this meeting?"

"It was fantastic! Fallon concluded the deal with us!" I look at the folder that stands in front of me. It's black and doesn't say anything, but its content is worth a hundred thousand dollars. I hold it more tightly between my fingers. Now everything is in order at last—a contract signed by Fallon is in the folder.

"Did you also notice any sales techniques?" Ed enthusiasm is contagious. "It is important that you understand them!"

"Objections! You dealt masterfully with their objections!"

"It was a very classic situation, Maggie!" Lewis sighs. "The closer it is to the moment of making the decision, the more objections a customer will find. It is human nature to doubt whether what they need anything, when the choice is almost made!"

"Why do we doubt?"

"Because the customers are afraid too! They will also have to leave their comfort zone! Changing their behavior is not easy. They will have to learn something new when they choose our system, and their fear tries to protect what they already know."

"Can we tell them that we know that they're afraid?"

"No, you do not want to make customer feel weak and defenseless. You have to convince them that the greatest security comes from being on your side! The best way to do this is to refute their objections. Address their objections one at a time. Take every complaint individually and discuss them all. Engage the customer and find out why they think the way they do. It is like standing in a tower—the building and the gardens are so big, but when you're at the top of the highest tower, you have a completely different view- point about what is going on. It is the same with the customers' fears and objections. Your duty is to provide the other viewpoint!"

"That is the value map!"

"That's right – by the way, after the meeting Fallon told me that he could not get the Board to agree to buy our CRM. Our arrival was auspicious, Maggie! It was the right decision! Aggressive, but correct!"

Aggressive, but correct.

"Ralph said that aggression is..."

"He is also aggressive! Sorry, that I interrupted you. Believe me, Ralph McCarren is the second most dangerous and unpredictable salesperson in Tamm after me! But here is the small difference—everything lies in the assessment of the situation, not the attitude! I need, and I ask you, to stand firmly on the ground when it is an appropriate situation, such as you just saw; but I would not tolerate it if aggression is used to pin the customer downs and they take *Tamm* because they have no other choice. We help, Maggie, not intimidate!"

Assess the situation, not the attitude. That's clear.

"I still want to praise you for asking us for help," the boss says. "We tell you that you have to learn and deal with many tricky situations, but never forget that you can ask for advice when you do not know what to do! Team work is in the genes of *Tamm* employees!" he reminds me. "This situation with Fallon was good enough to use my resources. You do not have to spend time on things that others can do better than you; it is my responsibility to deal with such situations!"

"Thank you!" I smile. "And thanks for not telling them that we had some inside information!"

"I would never do that! It's good to know such information, and sometimes it can be mentioned, but not this time. Why not this time? Because this information was not the reason why Metals LLC did not want to buy our *CRM*! As you saw, they had completely different objections. If we had mentioned that, it would not be ethical for any party involved!"

Information was not the reason why they did not want Tamm, I repeat to myself. *I need to remember this.*

"Maggie, what we need to do at the end of such dates?"

"Conclude a deal?" I guess, remembering Ed stretching his hand to Fallon. "To know their decision?"

"Yes!" Lewis turns onto the street, where Tamm Solutions' offices are located. "Today it was particularly important, because we were just introduced to Dauga! A handshake is one of the methods of concluding the deal."

"Why?"

"Because symbolically it means the same as signing a contract! Did you notice that Fallon hesitated? It is a great dilemma for the ego, especially for a man. You cannot refuse to shake the person's hand when it has been offered to you, but on the other hand you should realize that you have also said 'yes' to the deal. For Fallon that was extremely high pressure, which was strengthened by the fact that I said, 'we need to know the answer today!' The fate of the deal depended on one handshake!"

Ed parks the car in a parking garage, but I linger in memories of Metals LLC. *A handshake. Therefore, Fallon hesitated to shake Ed's hand. What would have happened if Fallon had not shaken Ed's hand? Would we have gone away without a contract?* And then I realized why a sale is a matter of chance, regardless of how certain the customer is about purchasing the product or service. We, as people, are subject to certain situations, experiences and feelings, and make choices according to them. We cannot predict anything. Shouldn't we worry than about what will be the outcome of the deal?

"Is there any other method of concluding the deal?" I ask, hoping that Ed will give me exact instructions that will provide me the desired result.

We get out of the car and go to the office.

"Of course, there are! There are many ways to conclude a deal. You must understand the customer and choose the method that works best for them! Today we used two methods—a handshake, and the authority of the boss. You can ask a coworker to conclude the deal in your place, if you foresee that there will be difficulties. Authority helps! You can use "the smart decision method," and flatter the customer, telling them that they have made the right choice. You can use "the calendar method," and schedule a date when to enter into a contract. Maggie, just remember that there is no universal recipe for concluding a deal!" Ed shatters my expectations. "Read the book *Secrets of Closing the Sale* written by Zig Ziglar, and you'll find many more interesting issues."

"Thank you, Ed!" I say as we enter the office. "And I'm sorry I could not help you much! I believed in you, but I was scared!"

"Are you afraid now?"

"No!"

"Do you know the main reason why we went there?"

"No," I shake my head.

"I asked you if Fallon fits Tamm. You said yes! Your confidence was enough for me to go over there and win him over for us."

I laugh and return to the sales office. There is no one there, and I let myself enjoy the silence and calm down. It was a real challenge! I sit down on the couch and look at the *Deals 40* sheet. Ralph has already marked two concluded deals. *Ralph McCarren is the second most dangerous and unpredictable salesperson in Tamm after me, but everything depends on the assessment of the situation, not the attitude,* Ed said. *I have so much to learn and so little time left!*

I look at the poster about the comfort zone and feel an irresistible urge to go over to it. I get up. *Does it really work?* I walk to the poster, checking that no one is watching me. I am not ready for a public participation in the mystic rituals of *Tamm Solutions'* sales team. Then I stand quite close to the poster. "A comfort zone is the most beautiful place—where nothing grows." *Nothing grows.*

I feel proud—today I feel far outside my comfort zone. I lift my hand and press it against the poster, so close that it leaves my handprint on it for a moment. I laugh and close my mouth with the other hand, so as not to let the sound out. "A comfort zone is the most beautiful place—where nothing grows." *How can we live in one at all?*

***

I have recovered, and thus the success that I experienced after meeting with Tom Audrins has also returned. I've paid my debt by bringing the doughnuts. Ed and I have agreed that we will start the implementation of Metals LLC's contract when Oliver Fallon is back from his vacation. I want to work, and to work hard and long. I want to reach the level where I no longer have to fear for myself and my skills!

***

"Do you have any contacts in the Design Trade company?" Carl asks Anna. "I want to write to creative agencies about *Tamm*, but I cannot find the information for this one. For the first time, I see that they have a website that is not very informative!"

I listen carefully. One of my friends works at Design Trade.

"Don't contact them!" I crane my neck and answer Carl.

"Why?"

"At least not now! Now they are going through a business reorientation process, and perhaps they will move to Italy. The main director has married an Italian, and it is reasonably certain that they will be moving."

"How do you know that?"

"A good friend of mine is working at Design Trade. That is my primary source of information."

"Thank you, Maggie!"

"No problem!" I wink.

Internal information. I run my fingers through my hair, again ascertaining why Anna thinks it is the best source for customers. I too have begun to build such a network.

Taking my notebook from the drawer, I check the calendar and the clock. My Friday one-to-one session with Ed starts in five minutes. I straighten the collar of my blouse and go into battle. This is the first session when I am not afraid. I knock on the door.

"Come in!" Ed says. There is a blonde woman wearing a white skirt and a blue blouse. I think that I have seen her before, but I cannot remember where. "Elsa, this is Maggie, our junior sales consultant. Maggie, Tamm's CEO, Elsa!"

I flush—of course I have seen her! I looked up profile of the *Tamm Solutions* CEO in *LinkedIn* several times before deciding to join the company!

"Hi!" We shake hands and smile. It seems to me that Elsa is older than her photograph.

"Maggie is responsible for the deal with Fallon!"

"Really?" Elsa blinks. "Good job! Talk to you later."

Elsa says goodbye and leaves us alone. I did not know that anyone from Washington was here in New York.

"I had exactly the same facial expression when Elsa came to visit me," Ed says. "She is particularly interested in the deal with Fallon. This is the first time we've had this kind of deal in the history of Tamm Solutions, so you can be proud of yourself!"

I smile.

"But with deals like you made with Stenne and Fallon, many people will expect more heroic deeds from you!"

Do I have to ask if I will still work for Tamm after my probation period is finished at the end of next week?

"Everything will depend on your KPI at the end of the test period, Maggie!" the boss continues, answering my question. "How is it going?"

"I've been busy!"

"Yes, I noticed that in the CRM system! You have cancelled five meetings. Why?"

"Their expectations have changed. Two immediately said no, and with the other three I'm still talking about changing the timing," I explain.

"How do you feel about it?"

"Neutral," I cross my fingers. "I do not want to worry about things that cannot be changed, so I just keep doing my work!"

Lewis smiles so slightly that he probably thinks that I have not noticed it. It confirms that I am doing the right thing.

"Have you asked for referrals to other contacts from those who said no?"

"Yes! I managed to reach one of them today."

"Well, Maggie! You're like quicksilver, I can't tell just what to expect from you. That's ideal for a salesperson, I would say!"

Amazing! Two compliments simultaneously!

"However, we must take care of your KPI. Ten transactions per month is a lot for a new salesperson. Sometimes this amount is unattainable even for experienced salespeople!"

The compliment has been diminished, and there is no place for flattery anymore. I sigh.

"How can I help you?"

"How can I work more efficiently? I was thinking that after the investment session I could communicate with the investment funds and other organizations that allocate funding for technology companies, such as accelerators. They always need to process a lot of information, and they have the money..."

"Do it!"

"I have a plan to call them next week, and also the investor who gave me his business card!"

"Don't plan to do it next week, do it now!"

"Now?"

"Yes, now! Now is the best time to do important tasks. Don't postpone until tomorrow what you can do today!"

"Isn't that so that on Fridays we are thinking about the weekend?" I ask him and immediately regret it - it is absolutely wrong assumption.

"Maggie, play with your time!"

"What?"

"Give me a sheet of paper!"

I open my notebook and pull out one page, feeling like I did at the beginning of my career in *Tamm* when Ed drew the basis of my profile case.

"Time is all that you have. Not a minute more, not a minute less! How can you work more efficiently? Consider your time!" Ed draws a circle in the middle of sheet and writes the word *Time* inside it, and the word *non-time* outside of the circle. "People have a tendency to do everything, just not what gives them results. Just as people do not listen, they also spend their time on non-time. And you will always have more non-time!"

"What is non-time?"

"Non-time? This is the time that we use for inefficient activities. We focus on minor tasks that do not generate money. We distract ourselves from our work and spend a lot of time in the kitchen, talking with our coworkers. We deal with several issues at the same time, the so-called multi-tasking, hoping that we will be able to do more, but the result is that we lose everything. We postpone tasks because do not want to do them or find reasons why we do not need to do them yet. We are lazy and look cat videos in the internet." Lewis writes each of the points outside the circle, by Non-time.

Well, I don't watch cat videos, but I do many non-time activities. I hope that I have become better.

"Multi-tasking?" I frown.

"Multi-tasking is a myth, it is an illusory panacea of unproductivity. When we will try to deal with e-mails, calls, and fill in the system at the same time, we split our attention into three parts. How can anything like that can work efficiently, if we do not pay full attention to any of the tasks? Maggie, what are the things you do at the same time?"

"I have my e-mail open when I make cold calls," I confess. It does not bother me.

"Doesn't e-mail put you off the rhythm when you are calling?"

"Slightly! Quite a bit!"

"Imagine that you have just one hour to calls everyone you intend to speak to, but you receive ten e-mails and you have to dedicate five minutes to answer each of them. How many customers will you call?"

I do not have an answer.

"None!" Ed answers. "And then you will not have enough time to be able to do it, so you have to wait for the next day. If this repeats during the following days, you will not get around to making any calls at all!"

I had not thought about it that way.

"Day planners are not meant for those who don't know how to plan their time. They're used to arrange your activities so as to bring you the greatest benefit! Those are activities you realize in *Time*," the boss points. "Maggie, what brings you the best results?"

"Focus!" I answer quickly. "Yes, maybe I do some multi-tasking, but I have always follow-up on my work! If any date is canceled, I use this time to prepare new contacts! I have to achieve my KPI, and I never want to see the green frog on my desk, so I try to do the most niggly works immediately after the morning meeting. And I remember about values and customers! I do not list any daily goals yet though; this is obviously the issue I have to work on."

"Very well, Maggie. This is the right attitude!" Ed gets up and goes to the window. "Please, at the end of each day when you set your goals for the next day, add me to the task, so I can see how you're doing."

I nod. This is a close check on my activities. *Perhaps Elsa does not want me to work here, although I have got Fallon for Tamm?* I drive away those thoughts and take a breath.

"Is there any other way I can save time and be more efficient?"

Lewis comes back to the table and gives me the just completed page. I review it and blink.

The words LOVE YOURSELF have been written down beside all the time activities.

"When we are planning our time, very often we forget to leave time for ourselves. Yes, during the work we also have to think about ourselves!" The boss sits down. "I'm not talking about your ambitions. I'm talking about your body! About lunch, adequate sleep, rest and the ability to say, 'that's enough I'm finished for today!' The last few days I noticed that you have been working very hard, but please, do not make yourself a workaholic, even if it seems great to you now. It's not! The body knows how to reply! If you burn out, nobody will benefit from it. Your KPI will come if you take care of yourself and your health!"

I disagree. I have so much energy that the time does not stand still.

"And, yes, it's true!" Ed puts his hands in pockets. "Please, keep this sheet. What are your further plans?"

I get up and smile.

"To do everything with the best ethics, and in a manner that creates gratification within you - both mentally and physically!"

Lewis squints, and I know that my answer does not satisfy him. Let it be! I have activities that must be eliminated from my daily plan, and I cannot linger any longer.

"Do you have any objections against me?" I stop in the doorway.

"Nothing that you already do not know. Maggie, keep working!"

A smile blossoms, and I say, "Thank you."

I was afraid, but I am no longer afraid.

***

I stiffen. My breathing has become very quiet, and I hesitate to make any movement. *I will sit in the corner and not make a sound. I have to get used to this.*

"Maggie?"

That's ok. You do not hear voices. Nobody is here. It is too early.

"Maggie?" Mr. Unbearable is talking in the background, and it gets more and more difficult to keep my poise. *How can he see me at all, from his heights?*

I bite my lip. *A little longer. Just a little!*

"Are you going to tell us?" Ralph is impatient.

"YES!" I yell across sales office, and quickly stand up. My adventure with risk capital funds has proven to be successful! Not only the investors from the investment sessions have approved the acquisition of *Tamm* at the first date, but also three others! During the week I have got four deals!

I ring the sales bell loudly, and its melody brings a euphoria. I love positive emotions, and I adore this bell! The more often I ring it, more often I want to ring it—it's like a drug that takes me around the world in five seconds. Immediately I record the new name of the new customer on the *Deals 40* sheet and see that I have moved into second position, after Ralph. Not bad but considering that Tamm's best salesperson delivers fifteen deals per month on average, I still have a long way to go in order to earn the monthly sales award.

"What is your secret?" Carl asks.

"Quality customers!"

"Maggie," Anna says, entering the room. I jump up. "Oh, sorry! Please come to Vizier!"

"Now? I have to send a couple of e-mails."

"They can wait. Please, join us!"

I shrug and follow my coworker. Ed and a dark-haired woman with a cold sore on her lip are in Vizier.

Head Office Blues

"Thank you for coming, Maggie." Ed is serious—threateningly serious, and it makes me uncomfortable. Anna closes the door and sits down next to me. "This is Ingrid, Tamm's lawyer." He introduces the strange woman, and I greet her. "What you will hear now is confidential, so I would appreciate it if what is said stays in this room. You and Anna will be the only ones on the team who will be informed about it now."

I swallow. *What is the matter? Why are we here?*

"*Tamm* has attracted an investment of three million dollars. This will be invested in improving our product, and the rest will be transferred for acquisitions in the Northern European market." Lewis hits the tips of his fingers on the table. "These investments will be made in anticipation of changes in the company's board of directors, and decision-making policies."

I nod to show that I am listening. *That's nice, isn't it?*

"One of the points of the agreement is the complete retention of the product in Tamm Solutions, meaning that the appearance, technical capabilities, and the performance of the product remains the responsibility of our emerging business development manager and our technical director."

How does this relate to me?

"... which means that customers will not have any other opportunities to influence our software other than by providing references to other customers. This means that customers will not have any rights to keep any specific function, created together with Tamm, only for themselves!"

Fallon. I give a weak cough. *That's why Elsa was here. Oh no! More trouble!*

"Maggie, the investment agreement will impose a veto on the Advisors program!"

"How? When? Why?"

After we have done so much work to save this deal, they are throwing us underneath a train. It is not fair!

"But why? This cannot be, Ed! Oh God, I promised! *I* promised that we would deliver *Tamm!*"

"Ingrid is here to help us understand whether Fallon has any legal protection..." Ed looks like an animal ready to be slaughtered. Even the mighty Ed Lewis is only a chess piece in the game played by the new investors.

"Ed, we have signed the contract!" I grip his hand. "Fallon will not leave it like this!"

"According to the information available to me, the Advisor contract has only been signed by Oliver Fallon," Ingrid says in business voice. *What does that mean?* "A contract only comes into legal effect when it has been signed by both parties. *Tamm* Solutions has not signed it yet, which means that Mr. Fallon has no legal grounds to require us to deliver a product or to recover penalties from us. No contract exists!"

This is terrible! I hope we will be able to find a way out. But I understand that this is a reality that cannot be changed. I press my fists together.

"And our reputation?"

"We will handle that! Don't worry. When Fallon returns from vacation, Anna will meet with him and explain everything. You will not have to do it."

Oh God, I promised. Do Ed and the new investors realize that we have bitten the hand that was ready to feed us? Incredible! I'll be raked over the coals on a fire made by Fallon. I promised him, and I have betrayed him.

Looking at Ingrid, Ed and Anna, I straighten my back. I will not participate in deals by default, based on the unclear decisions of company policy. Surely *Tamm* Solutions did not know about those investments beforehand! Ed would not have allowed all this to go so far that my future career as a salesperson could be threatened if Fallon decided to act on the cancellation of our agreement! It cannot be that the investors themselves are so narrow-minded that they do not see that the Advisor program could be beneficial for Tamm!

Either win or learn. Will that be the everlasting motto of the great sales guru? Ok, Ed, I'm still the quicksilver. I get up and leave Vizier. Everything I've done is worth nothing. The gene of the Tamm employee—does it actually exist? How crazy do you have to be to comply with it?

Finding Strength

I sit, huddled in the corner of the living room, and cry. How many mistakes can I make in one workplace? I cannot understand why failure is persecuting me in Tamm Solutions. I have called my mother. I need to hear a comforting voice.

"What do you think, can my dream job be a nightmare at the same time?" I sob in the receiver. *I want to be back at home and far away from the busy streets of New York. My small town, with its rows of pretty trees along the streets feels a lot safer, and I want to hide in their shade.*

"Dreams do not come easily, Maggie. You must fight for them! Dreams themselves can sometimes cause pain!"

"I think..." I wipe tears from my cheeks. "I think you were right about the fact that I am not the right person for this job... that I have much more to offer than just endlessly fighting against windmills! I feel... I feel that I have not made the right choice! I dream too much!"

"Maggie Kent, I do not like that you're a salesperson." My mom pities me, and I know that if she was here, I could find shelter in her bosom and fall asleep. "But that's my dislike, not yours. I have to live with it, not you! The only person you have to prove something to, is you! You have to prove that your dreams are not just empty words. Weed the roots out of the weeds!"

"What?" I become attentive. *Instead of encouraging me to leave, she is encouraging me to not give up?*

"Remember your apple tree? Are you the apple tree that you planted?"

"I don't know!"

"Well I know that you are! At the beginning your apple tree was weak and sickly, but now it is flourishing as never before, and this year will bring an excellent, not just good, harvest!"

I lean against the wall, imagining our apple orchard.

"So much fruit! This year your tree will be the star! When you go to work, you also think of fruits, don't you? About how much you will sell, to whom and what! The more fruit, the more gorgeous the tree, the more powerful you!"

Life is a tree, and I think of the fruit. About deals, all the time. Do I have dense foliage?

"But foliage is not composed only of fruit," mom continues. "There are also leaves, and they sometimes surround the fruits so that they cannot be even see. When the wind blows into the leaves, they sway and make noise. Does this make the trees less valuable? Although leaves create the noise, they are so green and rich; they supplement the foliage, not distort it! Daughter, the foliage is beautiful when it can grow and develop...when it is full of difficulties and beauty...when it aware that nothing comes easily in this life! Everything is always in balance, isn't it?"

Yes, I have leaves, I think. *They're lonely. Without flowers. Failures. Empty deals. Small deals. Incomplete deals. Overbid deals.*

"Yes."

"And what enables the foliage to be beautiful? You, daughter!"

I enable the foliage to be beautiful, I repeat to myself. *How?*

"You, daughter, are the trunk and roots! Everything that you do affects the foliage!"

"Mom!"

"Would it grow, without knowing how to? If it wasn't in the soil, what would help it? I have taught you, but you have got to go through the hardening yourself, facing challenges and moments of happiness. Your roots are your personality! Emotions. Thoughts. Prejudices. Habits. Education. Everything! Would you want to become a salesperson, if you had not seen your Grandma do it? Think about that!"

I want to sell the world to the world, I once told my grandmother when we were sitting in the market. *Do not forget it,* she said, *when the world will not understand the world.* My roots are as strong and thick as the largest oak in the village. I am the roots.

"Great trees always find a way out of the difficulties! Find a new branch, find where to go! Exactly the way your apple tree did it, daughter! The power lies in you, and you have a head on your shoulders!"

"Mom!" I growl.

"Yes, Maggie?"

"I love you!"

"Oh, Maggie Kent, if you only knew how proud I am of you! I am the happiest mother on earth! And you have not even released your true power!"

"My true power?"

"The true power that dwells in your heart! You do not need to learn to control it. You have to learn to cooperate with it!"

I smile. I imagine the wind in the apple trees, and the whole garden rustling in joyous unison. My mom's words have helped, and my hands do not tremble any more.

I was afraid, but I am no longer afraid.

***

I arrive in the office and touch the comfort zone poster. Ralph sees it, and smiles.

"Maggie, are you starting to believe in our superstition?"

"Perhaps," I throw him a mysterious smile. "I'm still checking how much!"

Mr. Unbearable nods, and I wink. Then I go over to Anna.

"I would like to apologize for my attitude!" I whisper in her ear. "It was a very unpleasant surprise, and I reacted inappropriately."

"That's ok." My coworker looks at me with understanding. I realize that it is not easy for her as well. The ability to say no must be ground like a diamond.

"How are you feeling?" I ask her.

"I will be ok. It's not the first time!"

She sighs. She has a meeting with Fallon on the Thursday after he comes back from his vacation, and after that everything will be complete and definitively decided.

I sit down at the table and find my notes. I stick the note saying "Sell the world to the world" on my profile case and get ready to begin my work. *How will Anna will say no to Fallon? How important is that the contract does not exist? Will the truth be enough for Fallon?*

Opening my calendar, I see five dates arranged for this week. That cheers me up. My enhanced time management skills have doubled my discipline. I check my tasks for today and whether I have added Ed to them and book the CSC for my post-meeting activities. *What will happen when I become a master? I will help so many others to be better in their businesses!*

"Good morning!" Ed greets the sales team in our morning meeting. I organize my desk, take out my notebook, and am ready to start. "Ralph, will you be the first?"

***

I pray for Thursday to come later than usual, but in spite of that it seems to come faster. I wish Anna good luck and look forward to a positive outcome. I remind myself that tomorrow will the last day of my probation period and I must do everything necessary to make *Tamm* keep me, but my thoughts keep straying back to Metals LLC and Oliver Fallon. Feverishly, I walk around the office. In the moments when I can finally concentrate and forget about my worries, I look at the *Deal 40* sheet where the name Metals LLC has been stroked out with a thick line. *I'm sorry that deal did not succeed.* I am extremely sorry. The phone rings, and I jump up. The screen displays Fallon's number, and I hesitate to pick up the receiver. It takes all my strength to answer this phone call.

"Hello!"

"Hello, Maggie, Oliver Fallon calling." His voice is angry. "I am sitting opposite Anna, and she has been telling me that the deal will not happen! Will you explain what this means?"

My pulse accelerates like a wildfire, and I gasp for breath, so I won't choke. *I was afraid, but I am no longer afraid. My tree is beautiful.*

"Mr. Fallon..."

"Is this some kind of a joke? Two weeks ago, you and Ed Lewis were here and swore for yourselves that this deal would go through. You, Maggie, you promised me yourself that we had a deal!" His anger increases with every word. I am imprisoned in a cage and I have to justify a crime that I did not commit.

"Excuse me..."

"Excuse you for what? For being a group of fools? Liars? Charlatans? What kind of authority do you have there if one employee says that the deal will happen, but another says that it will not? Do you even know what is happening in Tamm?"

"The contract has not been approved." I am grabbing the first thought that occurs to me. I'm not prepared for this and amidst the flames of the customer's anger I could cause even more damage. *Concentrate!* It sounds like Fallon would crawl through the receiver and strangle me, if he could.

"What is not approved? You double-dealers left with my signature! Does that mean nothing to you?"

"I..."

"I will ensure that nobody will ever use Tamm Solutions! NEVER!" Fallon threatens. I turn pale and grab the desk, so I don't fall. *Can he do what he is threatening?* "I have influence, and you know it, Maggie! I will tell everybody that you do not keep your promises! You cheated me! You cheated the Board! You are not a reliable partner, and this is not the end!"

Fallon slams down his receiver.

For at least a minute I sit frozen with the phone at my ear, hearing nothing more than hollow silence. I realize that his resentment speaks through him, and I cannot do anything to change this situation. *What shall we do? Oh God, Anna! She has to deal with it alone!*

I shudder and think about calling Fallon back. The Smart Customer needs to know that we did not want to harm him, and that this situation is a part of a completely unforeseen circumstance. I dial the number but hesitate to press the call button. My brain has boiled over from the excitement, although the only thing that I want is to help. *I will not call*, I tell myself, and put the phone back on the table. *It will not save anything*.

The End of Probation

Friday is my last day. My legs tremble, but I puff up my chest and raise up my head. I am wearing the same outfit as on my first day, and now we both expect a change. We have both gone into the sales profession and learned how things work. Although I started as a simple stone, I have been made into a jewel. I could use some more polishing, it is true, but I have learned a lot—and I hope that has been noticed.

I want to be a salesperson. And I want to sell the Tamm Solutions CRM. I believe what Ed has taught me and have made sure that a sale is more than a blunt imposition of the product on the buyer, and that we actually help people to become better. That's what my grandmother always said in the market, and what I did here on a daily basis.

Yes, I faced glowing, excited peaks of achievement and the deepest hell, but we salespeople are artists who have to live with that. We are artists with the anxiety, fear, creativity and ignorance that allows us to leave our comfort zones, because we like the flowers around us to blossom. Tamm Solutions is unsurpassed. I made mistakes and I learned how to present the value of our product to our potential customers. How to be confident and humble. How to really listen and ask questions. How to be wayward and still do my job. To fight. To be aware that we cannot control everything. And, I realized that salespeople are also afraid.

The *Deal 40* poster has been removed, and Ralph has been declared as the winner. His prize is a new clock, sitting in his jacket pocket. I remember where I finished and my KPI. Five deals and forty-nine dates are the final result of my test period, and I am worried about what Ed will say. *If he had not increased the number of KPI deals, I would have achieved my goal. Surely, he will consider that? What will I do if he doesn't? If my results are evaluated strictly by the numbers?* He has proved many times that his tasks are almost like laws, and not meeting the established KPI is definitely the greatest violation of all.

What will happen to me, if I do not get a permanent job at Tamm? Where will I go?

My success, even with unachieved goal, is valuable. I know that. I saw it in the eyes of the boss yesterday, when said goodbye. I made cold calls, met customers, I learned—I did not always succeed—but I was a salesperson without any experience and did almost the impossible within these last three months.

Work, like sales, is much more than just numbers. I have contributed to the team, and Ed must have noticed that. This can be proved not only by my success with Stennis, and my failures with Fallon and Tom Audrins, but also by the test of the Tamm employee gene—having fervor and courage.

I have to stay here, especially now with the new investments, *Tamm* will be introduced in other areas and they will need talented salespeople.

It is three o'clock, and I glance at my profile case for the last time. *Whatever the outcome is, I...*

I stop my thoughts and slowly go to the boss's office. I would like to linger for a moment before the decision is made. Right now, I still belong at Tamm Solutions. *Oh my God!*

I stop at the door and force myself to knock.

"Come in!" Lewis says.

I had not noticed that the doors of Ed's filing cabinet are gray with a small scratch in the upper right corner. *Those drawers are so simple, but behind them is my fate. They can allow me into my dream, or welcome me to a nightmare. Has any other salesperson realized the value of those drawers? Have any of them ever experienced the same tension, when the door, although their hand firmly holds the door-handle, does not open for them?* I close my eyes, make up my mind and enter the room. Ed is sitting in a chair and smiles, as if a friend has come to see him. That encourages me.

"Come in! Sit down! Maggie, we need to have a very serious conversation." His smile disappears, and the passionless Ed Lewis is in front of me again.

I sit down and take a breath. *Let's begin.*

www.ingramcontent.com/pod-product-compliance
Lightning Source LLC
Chambersburg PA
CBHW060822170526
45158CB00001B/58